Surviving Vietnam

Surviving Vietnam

Dennis Nickell

Diana Hershey-Nickell

The Second Mission Foundation

CONTENTS

Reviews of Surviving Vietnam — 1

Dedication — 4

Foreword — 5

Quiet Place — 6

Prologue — 7

1 | In The Beginning — 9

2 | The Purple Flash — 12

3 | School Days — 18

4 | Death and Destinations — 20

5 | Vietnam — 25

6 | Hopeless to Helpless — 29

7 | Hitting Bottom — 33

8 | Destiny and Diana — 36

CONTENTS

9 | Violence 40

10 | Going to the Chapel 44

11 | Under the Tree 49

12 | Job to Job 51

13 | First Business and First Baby 56

14 | Terra Bella 59

15 | Changes 64

16 | Trust 69

17 | Trials and Tribulations 73

18 | Homeward Bound 79

19 | Moving, Moving, Moving 85

20 | 'Round the Mountain 94

21 | Happy Thoughts 105

22 | Sinking Business 111

23 | Heart Attack! 114

24 | California, Here We Come! 118

25 | Happy Thoughts Store 122

CONTENTS

26 | Time is Everything 125

27 | Transitions 128

28 | VA 131

29 | Freedom's Cost 134

30 | Wellness 139

31 | Let the Games Begin 145

32 | Family 149

33 | The Gift of Jake 154

34 | "The Trish" 159

35 | Reroofing and Repairing 163

36 | Trial by Fire 168

37 | Friendly Fire 176

38 | The Gifts 182

39 | Highway to Hell 187

40 | Being Broken 194

41 | Letting Go 200

42 | The Nest 206

| vii |

CONTENTS

43 | Standing 212

44 | Thirtieth Anniversary 217

EPILOGUE: IF YOU ONLY KNEW 221

Reviews of Surviving Vietnam

"This is truly a story of redemption and of living through the toughest of circumstances throughout one's entire life. It is a sharing of the story of two people who truly loved one another and persevered against almost impossible odds. I had the privilege of meeting Dennis and Diana many years ago through a program my wife Pat and I sponsor called Horse Sense & Healing. The program was free for veterans, first responders, and people who have served their nation in wars and other catastrophic events causing their lives to be altered by what we call post-traumatic stress injuries. It was so rewarding to watch and experience Dennis going from practically unapproachable to an outgoing and happy individual learning to trust again through the help of horses. As outlined in this book, much of the credit for his transformation over the years is the steadfast support given by Diana and his family, as they navigated situations that most ordinary people would never have survived and come out the end as a winner. Despite the abject obstacles this amazing couple experienced along their life paths, it is gratifying that ultimately their enriched lives were uplifting with an end that leaves the reader with the feeling that no matter what life deals oneself, there is always a way to turn things around to become a positive. Dennis believed that every veteran should choose to fight for a better future."

~ *Monty Roberts, subject of the award-winning documentary "The Cowboy and The Queen" and author of "The Man Who Listens to Horses" as well as numerous other award-winning books.*

"One of my first experiences with Dennis was when he tried to settle a billing dispute with my father by asking to fight him in an alley. And that pretty much sums up the first decade or so that I knew him. When I think back on those days, I picture him walking around in a wife-beater tank top with his chest puffed out and a crazy look in his eyes, fists clenched and ready to go. If his reputation didn't precede him, you could tell just by looking at him that he was fighting some demons, and was probably best left alone. His youngest son, Israel, became one of my best friends, so I had a front-row seat at the drama that was Dennis' life. And like any production, that first act was merely setting the stage for a bigger picture unfolding in his life. While his crazy eyes never really went away, his demeanor softened over time and I ultimately came to appreciate the little nuggets of wisdom and encouragement he'd share every time I saw him. The adversarial fighting spirit that marred much of his life became one of his greatest strengths, *because he endured* for the those he loved. I am grateful to have known such a larger-than-life man like Dennis. If I hadn't seen it with my own eyes, I'd never believe his life story was true. But I did see it. And it is true. If a man like Dennis can find redemption and joy in his life, so can you. Be encouraged by his story. And don't quit."

~Sasha G. Pendergraft, RN, BJJ Black Belt, ADCC Head Medic

"A journey of a wounded warrior, his family, and the interwoven providential hand of a merciful, loving God, who is able to heal the deep-seated traumas that only Vietnam veterans would fully understand. A refreshingly transparent story of endurance, faith, love, and forgiveness, that imparts hope to those carrying pain with the awareness that no trauma is beyond healing."

~ Karin Clement, David & Karin Clement Ministries Founder.

"The trials and tribulations of life are marked by the rise and fall of the tide. The revulsion cast upon the Vietnam War veterans when returning home created more scars than the Viet Cong ever inflicted. Pressure to fight in an unjust war from a thankless country caused a rift between those who survived, and those who protested. Honor them with a podium to tell tales of hard-earned wisdom. Vietnam Veterans deserve a microphone, instead of medicine. Their insight can help struggling modern-day veterans cope with the betrayal from a country destined to destroy their spirit."

~ *Scott Chapman, featured author of* The Havok Journal *who served in Alpha Company 2nd Battalion 75th Ranger Regiment from 2001-2005.*

"I love Dennis and am extremely grateful for the time I got to hang out with him while he was here. I want to continue to share his story and how he helped me understand how to start to heal after dealing with war. He may not be with us physically anymore but he is and will always be in my heart and will continue to help combat vets through his stories."

~ *Joshua Martin, Army Sergeant with seven years of service including two tours to Iraq.*

"Dennis and Diana Nickell have blessed me more than I am able to share here in a few words. I am forever grateful for them -allowing themselves to be vessels of God's Grace. When I first met Dennis he had just had a heart attack. He had been warned by other doctors of his health conditions but was very distrustful of the medical profession in general. We were able to create a "relationship first" practice, one not based on fear, not based on authority or "top down" directives, but on care, understanding and transparency. This foundation helped us build a connection that fostered health and wellness. What a gift! To participate in the wellness of the men and women who have served in our military and encountered challenges reintegrating to "normalcy." Thank you Diana, and thank you Dennis."

~ Jorge L. Moreno, DO, is an accomplished osteopathic physician who is deeply dedicated to holistic healthcare and has positively impacted countless lives over his career.

Cover art by Isaiah Nickell

Dedication

This book is dedicated to Isaac, Isaiah, & Israel Nickell

It is said the goodness of God will lead people to him and children are referred to in scripture as a reward of the Lord. The gifts of our three sons, Isaac, Isaiah, and Israel were often our inspiration, and our happy thoughts. Being entrusted with such amazing souls I remember the day your father said immediately, this life is no longer about me, everything is about committing to the Lord, and raising my children to know Jesus.

Years flew by and as if these blessings were not enough, our sons' wives and nine grandchildren truly gave us a taste of heaven on earth. Thank you precious sons, Dad and I could not be prouder of each of you or love you more. So grateful we have eternity to share with you all.

–Dennis and Diana Nickell

Foreword

Sometimes, surviving the war is easier than surviving what comes after.

Dennis Nickell was a fighter. In his youth he graduated from childhood pranks to juvenile delinquency and eventually to the jungles of Vietnam. Along the way he lost his father… and began to lose himself. Returning from his combat tour he began to travel down a road that is all too familiar to warriors then, and now: a dark path of depression, substance abuse, and self-destruction.

But then, against all expectations, he met Diana. Diana was on a dangerous road of her own, but together they would begin a journey towards the light. Dennis and Diana eloped to Reno and then started fostering children as they began a family of their own. Although they never had quite enough money and their relationship was often rocky, they lived lives committed to others and together fought for a more-important cause: their family.

This is not the book you think it is from reading just the title. That's because surviving Vietnam–or any conflict–is as much about winning the battle on the home front as much as it is succeeding on the battlefield. And that's what this book is all about. For many veterans, of every conflict, making it home was the easy part; the hard part came after. Uniquely and masterfully told in turn by both Dennis and Diana, this book covers the ups and downs of life, love, and the fallout of war in a way that transcends time periods and conflicts. Ultimately, this is a story not of darkness but of the light of trust and belief in God, and the redemptive power of faith.

My own experiences in war are not from the jungles of Vietnam, but in the deserts of Iraq and the high plains of Afghanistan. But I feel connected to the themes evidenced in this book, and feel that military veterans, their spouses, and their families will feel the same connection in *Surviving Vietnam*.

–Charles Faint, veteran of the wars in Afghanistan and Iraq, owner of The Havok Journal and Executive Director of the Second Mission Foundation

Quiet Place

by Diana Nickell

Wanna go to a quiet place

Where pure and gentle hearts go to rest........

A stream dances by...

I see your eyes

Gotta tell, gotta tell the world

How much I love you

What you mean to me

I need you so

Did you have to go???

Tears fall on the inside like rain

I've tried to hide the pain...of losing you

Time stands still

But I will hold you again

Gotta tell, gotta tell the world

Whatcha mean to me

Prologue

by Isaiah Nickell

One of seven siblings born and raised in California's San Joaquin and Central Valley, Dennis Nickell–my father–lived a life that was anything but boring. Whether joyriding in stolen cars, hanging out with Hells Angels, or reveling in street fights, what he experienced in his youth turned out to be fun and games compared to the horrors that awaited him in the jungles of Vietnam. The war had already claimed the life of a high school friend, and an impulsive, revenge-driven decision to join the Army would result in a lifetime of consequences.

In *Surviving Vietnam*, Dennis tells not only his war stories, but the less often shared reality that combat veterans experience trying to go back to living a "normal life." A crippling drug addiction carried over from Vietnam, coupled with alcoholism as a coping mechanism to deal with the horrific PTSD from combat, formed the thin foundation that would barely allow this extremely angry violent man to survive.

Literally escaping from a psych ward of a hospital in Fresno, California and a diagnosis of paranoid schizophrenia from doctors who didn't yet understand at the time what PTSD was, Dennis found himself constantly in and out of homelessness, getting into fights, the drugs and alcohol not providing the relief he desperately needed. While staying at his mother's house, he hit rock bottom and finally gave in to the suicidal thoughts. A gun barrel pressed to his head, finger on the trigger, his mother arrived home early and unknowingly saved his life. Hearing her car in the driveway, he wasn't able to go through with it knowing she would find him that way.

Soon after this he would meet his future wife Diana and the course of his life would change dramatically. From a hopeless, homeless, drug addicted alcoholic to a married man with a beautiful wife and children that would give him something to fight for other than himself. Breaking free from those terrible addictions, he would go on to live a life full of actual miracles, carried by a faith stronger than anything he had ever experienced in his life. In his last few years, he would dedicate his time and energy to sharing his story on YouTube in his original series "Surviving Vietnam" with the sole purpose of stopping his brothers and sisters in arms from committing suicide.

Dennis believed that we all have the potential for a future so much greater than anything we can ever see at any given moment–a future that is always worth fighting for–regardless of our circumstances or how low we've fallen. He desperately wanted his fellow veterans to choose life and experience the unexpected joy and rewards that God is always ready to give.

1

In The Beginning

Dennis:

The love, peace, and joy that floods my spirit and soul have not always been there. Born fifth of seven children to Jack and Maurine Nickell, I never could have imagined the road ahead.

When I was 5 years old Mama herded all 7 of us kids onto a dusty old Greyhound bus that belched its fumes all the way from Seattle, Washington to Fresno, California. Dad had gone ahead of us and found a job as an appliance salesman at Sears.

Arriving in Fresno, Sandy, a woman I can barely remember, took in our whole family of nine until the day we moved to the projects. The projects were government housing for the poor. Now that I have a family and three sons, I know how special Sandy was. Taking in a family of nine is no small task.

The start of grammar school was uneventful. I did not consider our family poor, but I do remember having refried oatmeal for more than one breakfast. In school and out I was always running, which was helped by my closest brother Pat's love of chasing me. The fact that I called him names until he was provoked into it may have had something to do with it.

We lived several miles from the closest community swimming pool. On those blistering-hot summer days we would run and jump from grass patch to grass patch over burning asphalt to keep from burning our feet to get there. Collecting empty Coke bottles, we would sell those back to the stores to pay our way in.

One of the family's favorite outings was when all nine of us would pile into Dad's black and gold Nash Rambler station wagon and head to the airport. The ride was filled with anticipation, each of us trying to spot the first plane to come into view.

These were the nineteen fifties, the days of black and white TVs, no personal computers, and your family phone; it hung in one spot on the wall. Going to the airport was a really big deal in those days, and real entertainment.

The whine and vibrations of those huge engines as those big birds took off and landed right over our heads was truly thrilling. I had absolutely no idea, how airplanes and their destinations, would affect me in the future. Little did I know that in my future, a plane would take me to a place where my life would NEVER be the same.

On our outings in the car, Mama had a unique way of keeping control of seven children even though she was in the front seat. Her method was a much-feared "fly-swatter" which would deliver a sting that would quiet any kid. It kept her from constantly screaming at us too. Dad, on the other hand... in frustration, was liable to throw his sandwich or anything else he could get his hands on, out of the window.

Dad worked hard six days a week in sales and rarely got time off. When he did, he managed to take me fishing. I believe those were the closest times my father and I ever had.

When I was in third grade, Dad brought home the news that we would be moving. Although Mom and Dad had to be happy to move, we were sorry to leave many friends behind. Soon, however, we had enough friends to play street football at the new home.

Behind our house in Tarpy Village was a big vacant lot. It was dirt, with plenty of weeds and potholes. The lot was a perfect baseball field, which we dubbed "Nickell Stadium." A small plywood scoreboard nailed to a fence, in full view of passers-by, proudly proclaimed the name.

Meanwhile Mamma worked full-time at Woolworth's trying to help support a large family. Although a necessity, it left plenty of free time for me to get into everything and anything I could.

2

The Purple Flash

One of my new friends was Danny Hughes. I met Danny while going steady with his little sister Elaine. Danny was a year older than me. He had a get-a-way in the family garage, which had been partially converted to a room. One day I heard my name being called. "Dennis, come over here."

"No!" said Elaine, "He just wants you to try those awful cigarettes."

If I'd only listened! What seemed like a boyhood prank led to 24 years of being hooked. Not only that, but also the beginning of a friendship which ended up in some dangerous places.

One boring afternoon Danny and I decided that we needed a raft of some sort to ride down the canal behind his house. Danny's dad helped us tar some big dresser drawers so they would not leak. With the raft, some magazines, and plenty of cigarettes, we had our answer as to how to spend the rest of the day.

With the aid of my brother Pat, stealing candy and cartons of cigarettes became a favorite pastime of mine. The game was to see who could get the most at one time. One day Pat and I were at our favorite store when the owner caught Pat with a carton of cigarettes. Thank God, I had not shoved any candy bars down my pants yet!

Mumbling "See ya at home," I split. We thought the police had been called, but mercifully the store's owner just called Mom and left the punishment to the folks. When I got home that night all Mom said was, "Hit the bedroom." Boy, were Pat and I scared!

When Dad got home, we heard him bellow: "Pat, come here!" I thought for sure I was in for it but was tremendously relieved when all I got was a lecture. After the big talk, Pat and I left the local grocery stores alone.

"The Purple Flash" was the name of Danny's '49 Studebaker. It was the weapon used to terrorize the Clovis Police Department. "Go, Danny GO!" I shouted excitedly, as we raced down the canal banks throwing dust in the faces of patrol cars. High bumps caused the back seat, where I was hiding, to fly up and slam me on the floorboard. It would have hurt had I not been laughing so hard. The favorite get-away was to race up a street, slide around a corner and ditch into any open garage and slam the door shut.

Our hearts pounding in our chests, we would jump out, and walk to the nearest pool hall to shoot pool. It amazed us that we never got caught by any homeowners or police. Even more amazing was the way Danny's dad kept him in old clunkers while he was in seventh grade.

After a long hot summer, junior high school reared its ugly head. At the time, I had pictured it much worse than it really was. My fears were a combination of the fact that I was slight in frame (okay...downright little) and I was terrified of being rejected by the crowd.

Prepared for the worst, I began this new experience with attire that would please any girl of those days. My Levi jeans were so tight I was glad I had a skinny comb. The T-shirt I wore was decorated by a pack of "ciggies" neatly rolled up in one sleeve. To top it off, my hair sported the biggest pompadour you ever saw, complete with handfuls of pomade smeared through it.

I soon discovered dances were held every Wednesday night at Einstein Park and this turned out to be an opportune time to mingle with the wrong crowd. At the time it seemed like anywhere or anytime violence was happening, when provoked, I was the first one in. I had a cocky attitude to go with my small frame, and though I rarely started a fight, I would defend my friends with my fists in a minute.

"Hey, Dennis! Meet me over at Cedar Lanes," Wayne would say. Cedar Lanes was a bowling alley, which was the local hangout for Hells Angels. The attraction for the bikers was the pool tables there. Being young, we were intrigued by these tough-looking guys with their chopped bikes. Wayne and I started hanging out around them and soon they took a liking to us.

I remember there was a jukebox there, one of the big old-fashioned ones and they would play their favorite songs. I would jump on top of the pool table and dance with one of their "mamas." These big old guys would down their beer and laugh away. They liked that I was so cocky even though I was so small.

Grasshopper was the Hells Angel that took me under his wing. He was the president of the Fresno Chapter of the Hells Angles, but one day he disappeared—he went to the joint. No one told me what for, and I never found out.

When the Hells Angels weren't in, we would either bowl free or eat free. It was like a Peter Sellers movie. Wayne and I would scope out the booths and see who was eating what. As soon as people left a table, with leftovers to our liking, we would run and duck under it. From there, our hands could sneak up over the table edge, before the waitress could get there, and yank the steak or hamburger down to where we were hiding. Not exactly suave, but it did serve the purpose when we didn't have money for food.

Although I had many girlfriends in grammar school, junior high brought a girlfriend that truly won my heart. Robin was blonde, blue-eyed, and looked every bit like a Barbie doll to me. I gallantly fought another boy named Steve for fair Robin's hand and won.

As the huge crowd that had congregated watched, she took my hand and we headed towards her home. "Wait up," said Steve who had lost the fight. "What do you want?" I answered. "Can't I just walk with you and Robin one last time? Please?" Being the nice guy at heart, I said, "Okay, but only if you walk behind us." I felt bad, as he cried the whole way.

Little Anthony singing "Tears on My Pillow" was the backdrop for Friday night skating. Wonderland was the name of the roller rink and after skating until 10PM the real fun, and the sock-hop, began. Rows of Beatle boots, penny loafers and big-heeled shoes lined the walls. On more than one occasion when you asked a friend to watch your shoes, he'd go dancing, and when you got back-your shoes were gone!

I had naturally jet-black hair and wanted half of it to come out blonde. I went over to Danny's house and had his sister peroxide half of my hair. As Elaine rinsed out my hair, I knew something was wrong. With a wet towel around my shoulders, I looked in the mirror. To my horror, one-half of my dripping hair was a vibrant tangerine orange. It was the brightest, ugliest thing I had ever seen. This was in the 1960's.

At school the very next day, my mechanical drawing teacher, who I really respected, walked up and said, "Nickell, that's the most asinine thing I have ever seen!" That day when I got home, out came the razor and off came all the hair that had made up the biggest, finest pompadour at school. Now, bald, I wore a beanie to school.

One weekend the whole crew, including the "fly-swatter," went for a ride. Forty-five miles later we drove into the small town of Visalia. Driving by Redwood High School, we older kids joked that there was no way we'd be caught dead going to a school like that. Past the school and on down the quaint little main street sat Sears. You guessed it! Dad got a job at the Visalia Sears and our world was turned upside down.

A new town meant new friends, a new school and even more, having to build a whole new reputation. Right away my brother Pat was singled out at school for the way he walked. His walk looked cocky; and since Pat didn't think so, more than one argument was had over the subject. With that walk, our reputation was on the line. Being the new kids from out of town didn't help much either.

Right by the school was a hamburger joint called Gig's. Red and white striped, it looked like an ice cream parlor. Pat and I went there for lunch one day and a kid named Raymond offered Pat a Coke. Since Raymond was such a big kid, we figured why not? Well, he had the Coke ready and it wasn't until Pat took a mouthful that he discovered the guy had peed in the cup. To make matters worse, a crowd had knowingly watched, then had a good laugh at Pat's expense.

The next day while walking past the Safeway, which was close to the school, Pat spotted good old Raymond! He calmly walked up to the parking lot and said, "Man, why did you pee in my Coke?" Ray just laughed and Pat proceeded to deliver a good punch. Ten stitches in the mouth is what it took to repair it and this time, no one standing around was laughing. "Anyone else want some action?" I yelled. No one stepped up, but this was by no means the end of our troubles.

Known for its race riots, Redwood had plenty of violence between the Chicanos and the Whites. To follow suit, I found the weirdest, craziest guys I could hang out with. The challenging spot was a long cement wall with lots of Chicanos that squatted while balancing on their ankles. The bravest honkies would walk closer and closer till a Chicano was finally bumped, or his shoes were accidentally stepped on, then the fight would be on. Girls shrieking, people running, canes flying, you name it. Finally, since weapons were getting nastier and nastier, plain-clothes policemen were brought in to bust those with dangerous weapons.

One time, my friend Kenny Ray, was minding his own business in crafts class, when a group of Chicanos sauntered in with baseball bats and chains. Crack! A bat came down on Kenny's head, leaving a huge knot, and the craft teacher jumped on the attacker's back, trying to tackle him. Instead, he ended up being piggybacked all over the room.

This led to a counter- attack. Gangs of Whites met at Foster's Freeze and cruised en masse from there to the Oval, a gathering place on the north side of town. Armed with eggs, Coke bottles, clubs and yes, guns, we were ready for action and all hell broke loose.

From what I recall, two people were shot, and no one knows all the wounds suffered that day. A 1957 gunmetal gray Chevy was what I was riding in with the driver, Danny. After the fighting, we talked to one of our guys who had been shot, and we swore to get the sucker who shot him. We never could find out who did it.

3

School Days

A deep maroon 1964 Chevy Impala Super Sport was one of the rides I was seen around town in. My interests had expanded from violence and girls to a love of low-riders. My friend Butch had a cool older sister named Carol. She had some money, but no knowledge of cars so Butch and I picked out that Chevy Impala for her. She made us a deal that we could not refuse.

"Butchie, if you and Dennis will keep this car waxed up and in shape, I'll let you use it when I'm not." "Great!" was our reply. Carol had a steady who kept her busy every weekend, and we knew the car was ours for the weekend.

Around this time, I picked up a dark black '56 Chevy. Before I bought it, it had been used for racing at Raisin City. With a 350 engine and three speeds on the floor, it was something else. With access to plenty of wheels now, I started spending my weekends up in Fresno, my old stomping grounds. There I met Vickie, who was the most beautiful girl I had ever seen. She could easily have been a model, and she was really sweet.

While dating Vickie, I was practicing yet another trade. I guess you could say that I had developed an interest in the automobile industry. Ronnie, a friend of mine from junior high, carried a chain, which held about every kind of car key imaginable on it. "What kind of car would you like to go cruising in tonight?" he would ask. My favorites were

GTOs and Corvettes. This is not one of the things I got caught for, but I frequently did for others. I had been in and out of juvenile hall many times already, so Dad was leery about any friends I would bring around. He really sensed something about Ronnie. One day while Ronnie was visiting, he called the police and had them run a check on him. Boy, was I surprised when they arrested him right there in our living room.

Ronnie had felony warrants on him for stealing cars. At the time, I felt so betrayed by Dad, not to mention how Ronnie must have felt. Come to think of it, he pretty-well verbalized how he felt on the way out the door.

The latter years of high school were spent ditching. Mr. Scott, the dean of boys, once told me that I had the all-time school record for truancy. My sister Penny (yes, Mama actually- named one daughter Penny Nickell, who was called "Six Cents" for short would write my excuses. She wrote so many for me, that one day when I had a real note from Mama the school sent me home and wouldn't accept it, because they thought it was forged.

One day I cussed out the art teacher and he was so furious; he literally ran all the way to the office to ge t th e de an. Mr . Sc ott came to find me. With disgust, he looked at me and said "Nickell, why don't you go home and don't come back until you're ready."

"You gonna call my parents?" I asked.

"I won't even call your parents. Just do me a favor-go home and give me some peace."

Home it was for three weeks, then I returned only to keep ditching. I hated school.

4

Death and Destinations

My senior year only brought more pain. Butch and I were asleep in a little room built in the garage. when suddenly, my mother awakened us.

"I've taken your Dad to the hospital." I could tell that she was trying to fight back tears to be strong for me. "He's had a heart attack. They told me there was nothing I could do, so go on home. If they have any news, they'll call."

At 17, I just laid there for a minute not realizing the seriousness of a heart attack. Dad had never had any heart trouble. He was overweight, and yes Dad enjoyed his beer and cigarettes, yet I had no idea that could bring on a heart attack. What I did sense was that Mom was trying to be strong and managed to hide the pure terror that she must have felt.

Butch and I got up and comforted Mom, and at 6:00 a.m. the phone rang. A nurse from the hospital told Mama to get down there fast. Grabbing my younger brother Billy, he, Mom, and I raced to the hospital. Mama screamed frantically at traffic while I ran red lights and tried to shove down the terror.

When we got there, I must have sensed something, because I told Mom and Bill to go in, while I parked the car. Waiting a few minutes in the car, I got out and headed for the door. Halfway across the parking lot I was met by Mom who gave me the paralyzing news.

DAD DIED! He was GONE! I've never, before or since then, felt such pain. There are no words to express it.

Violence turned out to be my release for the pain. Running across the street from the hospital, I ran to a tree and just kept punching and punching it as hard as I could. Mom, always thinking about us kids, ran over and grabbed me to make me stop. Still trying to fight the tears, she said we would have to be strong for the rest of the kids. Jack, Sherry, Cathy, and Pat were all either married or moved out, but little Penny and my younger brother Bill still lived at home. Stunned, I can't remember the ride home, but the next few days were the worst in my life.

Memories of shining Dad's shoes as an anniversary present just weeks before came to mind. It was the nicest thing I had done for him in a long time. We all went down to the funeral parlor at different times, and I must admit Dad looked peaceful. To me the whole thing was like a dream. I'm sure I was in shock as was the rest of my family. The funeral was a final crushing blow to my heart, leaving scars to this day.

I graduated, if you could call it that, in 1968. I didn't give two hoots about the ceremony and three weeks before the big day, I went to see Mr. Scott. "Do I have enough credits to graduate?" I asked.

"Just enough," said Mr. Scott.

"Well, why not let me have my certificate now?" I asked.

"All right. Good luck in life." He seemed almost relieved to get rid of me.

I finished school three weeks early. I have the sneaking suspicion that Mr. Scott celebrated that night. Oh, he liked me enough, he just didn't agree with the way I did things… or should I say, didn't do things.

After working at the local car wash with Butch part of the summer, we decided to join the Army. A friend of mine had been killed in Vietnam and I was going to make somebody pay. The two-year buddy program was what the recruiter signed us up for. Talk about naive! My idea to make someone pay was not related to any reality about what going to war meant.

The easiest part of joining the Army was the paperwork. Getting there was another story. The night before I was to report, I was arrested and thrown in jail for public intoxication and disturbing the peace.

The next morning my mother, as only mothers can, marched into the sheriff's office and demanded my release. "You let Dennis Nickell out of this jail!"

"What was that lady?" the receptionist said in disbelief.

"You heard me," Mama stated. "My son enlisted and is now the property of the United States Army and you have to let him out."

After phoning the Fresno recruiting office, they verified that what my mom said was true. I was released. Freed. I was told later that the Army had said let him out now or we'll come and get him. Poor Mom, she thought I looked so bad she asked me if the cops had worked me over.

"Oh, son, did they hurt you?"

Laughing, I replied "No, Mom. Let's go."

One thing about Mama, even though her kids were far from perfect, she had a killer instinct when it came to protecting one of her brood. We could do no wrong in her eyes!

Boot camp was at Fort Ord, California. The system was easy for Butch and me to figure out. DIs or drill instructors meant business. All you had to do was follow all of their directions. For such a little word, "**ALL**" carries a big meaning. I was terrible at following directions and never did what anyone told me. Thank God, I had Butch to help me. I decided to do whatever Butch did and everything worked out.

After basic training we headed for Fort Sill, Oklahoma. A traveler may have thought "how adventuresome." But in truth, it turned out to be the coldest place I'd ever been. The cold felt like thirty degrees below zero at times; and if you were familiar with Army training exercises, you would know it was not fun.

One night I was supposed to be standing guard duty. It was so cold I crawled into the rim of a five-ton truck and fell asleep. The officer of the day drove up and caught me sleeping, which was really a godsend, as I could have frozen to death. After a minor slap on the wrist, I was informed that had I been in Vietnam at the time, more than likely my throat would have been cut.

By February my advanced infantry training, as it was called, was over. To tell the truth, I had about enough of playing "Army." Butch got his orders and lucky for him they said Korea. I thought for sure that I would follow him. Well, my orders were delayed; and I'll never forget saying goodbye to my best buddy.

Watching that taxi drive off until it was out of sight, I felt painfully alone. Butch was always there when I needed him. Everything inside of me yelled "Go AWOL!" Somehow I managed to hang in there a couple more weeks.

Then with trembling hands, I opened my letter, with those all-important orders inside. **Vietnam**! Now I knew I was through playing "Army." At 18 years young my sites were laid on the next good party, not a real war. Off I went totally ignoring all my responsibilities and headed for home.

While I had been at Fort Sill, Oklahoma, I received a letter from my mom saying she had remarried. The lucky guy was Dad's best friend, Gene Brown. He and his wife Betty had been pals with Mom and Dad for years. Shortly after my Dad died, Betty, Genes' wife discovered she had leukemia and within a few days was dead.

Out of their horrible loss, Mom and Gene comforted one another, and that led to marriage. Knowing that Mom must be tired of the loneliness, I more than heartily approved. I continued down my reckless path, but soon ran out of time and money.

One Sunday afternoon at a family get together my stepdad Gene called me aside. Gene was a veteran of WWII and though not in love with war, was concerned that I should want to defend my country. By now the United States officially at war with Vietnam. Respecting Gene, who had always been like an uncle to me, I did some thinking. Deep down I knew I must go. Soon after that I said my good-byes and contacted the Army.

Several family members and I took the drive up to Oakland. Joking and laughing the whole way, I fought back a rising uneasiness. When we got there, I unloaded my duffel bag and waving, watched everyone drive off. Suddenly, a crippling fear grabbed hold of me. I didn't know one single person there. Butch was long gone to Korea and friends and relatives were safely headed home. For the first time in my life, I was totally alone, not only alone but headed for war.

Lying around Oakland for a week gave me plenty of free time to consider going AWOL again. Things got a little better after I met a few guys. Then my name was called.

Boarding the plane my thoughts returned to the days as a child when I watched the big DC10s land at the Fresno airport. This time it was far from thrilling and had I known what lay ahead I don't know if I would have gone. The plane ride was thirteen hours long with stops in Hawaii and Guam. *What a difference your destination makes.*

5

Vietnam

I arrived in Ben Hoa on the 27th of March 1970. Stepping off the plane, the heat was so intense I could hardly draw in a breath. The next of my senses to be attacked was my sense of smell. Only someone who has been there can genuinely appreciate it.

The Vietnamese burned all their garbage, including human waste. I thought I would vomit from the stench. With the smell of burnt sewage burning my nose, and a heat I could barely move in, I hardly believed what my eyes were seeing. The "grunts," as they were called, looked like absolute maniacs. The name applied to infantry and others who had been in the bush. Stunned, my ears picked up chants from the vets who were headed home.

"Hey, Cherry Boys," they yelled, picking us out by our brand-new fatigues. "You left your mama at home! You better say awake over here or you won't see your mama ever again."

Wishing I was in a dream, I continued to scan the grunts around me. These guys had machine gun rounds draped around their necks as if they were necklaces and jungle hats of all different shapes and sizes, with hand grenades clipped to the front of their shirts. To top if off, some had adopted live jungle monkeys that leered from their shoulders and others had opted to drape themselves with giant pythons. **REAL PYTHONS!** Waiting for my orders from this holding place, stories of the GIs who hadn't made it out alive rang in my ears.

My third day in-country, a brand-new GI was pulling guard duty. He was smoking a cigarette when a sniper, who had focused on the glow, shot him. At that time, I smoked, but for the rest of my active duty, I never openly smoked after dark. I now knew this place was for real and played for keeps.

Transferring numerous times, I served with artillery units and airmobile units for the Ninth and Twenty-fifth Infantry, First Cav and the First of the 82nd Infantry. I never received any pay upgrades or rank that I know of. Sometimes, we would convoy into the jungles and at other times we were dropped in by helicopter. I spent all but my last 40 days in the bush.

Dennis in Vietnam

During this time, I became close to several "soul brothers" who were of the Black Panther persuasion. When I first met them, I wondered why I had gotten the meanest tattoo I could find, put on my arm, for the whole world to see while in high school. It is a huge Black Panther's head, with a dagger stuck in it with blood dripping down its face! Wonderful!

God spared my life through several close calls and with every day being blanketed with fear, many of us looked for ways to escape. For many, drugs were the way. Scag (liquid heroin), liquid speed, opium joints, and Cambodian red, to name a few, were readily available. Equipped with my own pipe and a candy dish full of weed I got loaded a lot of the time. Once a full bird colonel smoked dope with us as everyone tried to cope with being in hell any way they could.

One of the most talked about subjects among the men were two planes. Both those big birds would slowly fly over. One was the "FREEDOM-BIRD!" headed for home with GIs aboard. They all fervently prayed to make it past the border without getting shot down.

The other was the big "BLACK DEATH" plane, a sober reminder that there were no guarantees of tomorrow. No matter what we were doing, I seemed to notice when one or the other could be spotted.

Finally, I ended up going home, leaving from Cam Rhan Bay.

Remembering my first day there, I walked over to a recruit, but instead of calling him names I said to him, "Good luck and stay awake. This place is for real. If you pay attention and don't fall asleep on guard duty, at night, you'll make it." I wonder sometimes if that young man made it home.

As we were landing in Fort Lewis, Washington I cannot remember being more excited. It was the moment that I had dreamt about for fourteen long months. I'd really made it through war alive! Little did I know the price to be paid for going to Vietnam was far from over.

Dennis (R) and his Army buddies in Vietnam

I don't think I've ever smelled such fresh, clean, beautiful air, before or since. Yes you'd better believe it; I kissed that American soil before I walked on it.

An immediate briefing was held on our arrival explaining the discharge procedures. Some GIs still had active duty left but since I had chosen to do extra time in Vietnam, I was getting out for good! The first thing I did was call Mom.

"Oh, Dennis! Where are you?" she cried into the receiver.

"I made it! I made it! I'll need to be picked up at the airport in two days."

On the plane ride to Fresno a lot went through my mind; and I remember being extremely nervous. Worrying about the way I looked, I thought back to high school when I had a flawless complexion. Now, my face was solid acne! There was a time in Cambodia when we had gone without showers or even water to wash up with for over three months. The combination of red clay, mosquito repellent and sweat from the climate had ground into my pores and left its mark. The other main change in my appearance was skinniness, due to all the drugs and bad diet. As my pride was suffering, I wasted no time in getting bombed on the plane.

As the plane taxied slowly up the airstrip, I saw my friends and family anxiously waiting. Peering through the window I decided to play a little trick on them. Waiting while all the other passengers got off, I continued to peek at my family. Pretty soon they all looked panic-stricken.

With the stage set, I made my grand entrance popping out the door. My oldest brother, Jack, spotted me and let out a whoop! Yelling, we ran to each other and loving relatives mobbed me. It was great seeing everybody. Downing a handful of whites, the post war celebration began.

Debbie, a girl I had dated from high school, was the one I had been writing to from Vietnam. She'd gotten pregnant by someone else while I was away; but convinced me that he was long gone. I was so hurt, but figured she was entitled to a mistake; so, I called her and met her at a party. The party went on for several days, but when the excitement wore off, things were just not the same.

6

Hopeless to Helpless

With money in hand saved from Vietnam, my efforts were concentrated on finding a car and a place to live. Visiting Danny one day (remember Danny?) I saw this beautiful low-rider Lincoln Continental. It was solid white, had spoke wheels and the interior was powder-puff blue. Paying Danny only $700 for it, I now owned the ultimate low-rider. The only drawback was the low miles to the gallon it got. With my car situation taken care of now I just needed a place to live.

One day my brother-in-law, Johnny, mentioned his two other brothers had an apartment together. Their names were Rick and Garland; and hitting it off, I moved in with them. After a while, Garland needed more space, so he moved out. Quickly I learned that Rick was into drugs and in no time at all we were both strung out on uppers. Figuring we were saving money on groceries by living off of drugs, we started selling drugs to support our habits.

In Vietnam I had self-medicated with weed and heroin, dropped uppers, downers, and drank alcohol to deal with the war inside of me. Being home didn't stop the fear and searching for relief was now my new focus. Trying new drugs such as mescaline, paper acid, and peyote buttons didn't work either. My brother, Jack, was studying about drugs at Fresno State and came by several times to warn us about the dangers.

Rick and I laughed and invited him to take some. We wanted him to know it really felt like heaven not hell. We would even round up Coke bottles to buy the stuff. One night, I blew it bad. Really bad! Rick and I took a lot of whites and decided to drop some acid too.

One minute we were walking down Blackstone in Palo Alto tripping out on the lights, skipping along like you do when you are on acid. Coming to our street, we took off running as fast as we could. Coming to a stop, I got a rush that I thought would blow my head clear off the top of my shoulders. It felt like being startled, and then magnify that feeling of fear a million times.

"What's wrong?" Rick asked. I screamed something about losing my head and freaking out. The very fear I was trying to escape from was now worse than ever. Every day it got worse instead of better.

All the talk about drug-related suicides kept running through my head. A couple of days later, I decided to go to the Veterans Hospital for help. When I got there, I received a barrage of questions, which reeked of a third degree. They had no idea in 1971 what post-traumatic stress was, and neither did I.

Pumping me full of Thorazine, I was admitted to the psychiatric floor. This was the seventh floor, referred to as the "Nut Ward" by staff and patients alike. The therapy they started me on consisted of a steady diet of 25mg of Librium every 4 hours along with some Mellaril and Valium.

After an observation period, a panel of psychiatrists and psychologists and various doctors reviewed my case. They decided I was dangerous and crazy and prepared to ship me off to a mental institution for the criminally insane. They pegged my problems on Vietnam. Let me tell you, I was really freaked out. I now had a clinical diagnosis of paranoia, anxiety, and an inability to even take treatment. My destination was supposed to be some mental institution in Fresno.

When I realized what was happening, I planned and carried out "The Great Escape!" Dressed in my little green hospital pajamas with little matching green slippers, I made a mad dash to the elevator. The long seven floor descent remained uneventful. With all the composure

I could muster, I strode past the opening elevator doors as if I were a doctor or something.

Marching past the admissions desk and out into the bright sunlight, my eyes darted back and forth to make sure I wasn't being followed. My heart racing, I walked five miles across town, to my friend Jake's house, yep, FIVE miles across town in my pajamas.

My friend Rick was at Jake's and was concerned about where I was going to go. As the hospital hadn't helped, and I started drinking. The conversation turned to whose fault the whole thing was and I started blaming Rick. Angrily, I threw anything I could at Rick and a glass that I had just broken made good ammo and Jake's wall a good target.

Next I tried to fight Rick, but he knew I was drunk, and didn't want anything to do with it. Running outside, I found a defenseless bush and beat it with my fists, while I cried my head off in sheer frustration at the fear that would not leave me.

The hospital's treatment regimen of Librium and Valium replaced street drugs, but since I left that behind, I needed a pain reliever of some kind. It didn't take long to find out that booze was my answer. Man, the alcohol just made me more wild and violent than ever before. I was a walking time bomb.

One time, a guy kicked my friend's car. I kept a .45 pistol under my car seat, and my friend had a rifle. We drove to this guy's house. The lights were on inside the house and we just started shooting up this guy's car. We didn't stop there though; and we blew the heck out of his house, never thinking about what we were doing.

Bar fights continued for years. Barbiturates (reds), along with the booze, helped to fight my fear. But the fear was never completely gone. I made some return visits to the Veterans Hospital through the years, but never could find real relief.

One time I visited the VA emergency room with a broken hand with shattered knuckles. I told the doctor I had hit a wall, he looked me right in the eye and said, "Someone's jaw, you mean." Another time I went in with a human bite on my chest. I told the doctor that a dog had bit me and he said, "Nice try, but that's a human bite, and it's worse than a dog's bite. You might have died if you hadn't come in."

One bar fight stands out. It was when I challenged some huge maniac while I was on reds. "Shoot me!" I shouted in his face. So, he whipped out his gun and started firing. The wall behind where I crawled had numerous bullet holes; and I couldn't understand how he had missed.

By now I was a jobless drug and alcohol addict, full of violence and not very welcome at most my relatives' homes for more than a quick meal. Living in my car, I was such a wreck. I had absolutely no interest in anything, not even girls or parties. I was possessed with fighting the fear that gripped me. Since booze was my answer, it became the most important thing in my life.

7

Hitting Bottom

Getting money to buy booze was my motivation for starting college with VA funds. I stayed with Mom and Gene in Merced for about a year while going to school. Thank God for their help and understanding. They lived only a half a mile from the closest bar, which was attached to a bowling alley. One night I was there drinking and stayed till they closed. Walking home I ended upside down in an empty canal two miles in the opposite direction from Mom's. Waking up I had absolutely no idea where I was or how I got there.

Mom and Gene, "Pop," moved up near Redding, California after Browns Shoe Company transferred him. They moved to a mobile home park right on the Sacramento River, in a small town called Anderson. Since they had a big beautiful mobile home, they invited me along. They could see I was totally dysfunctional, and they wanted so very badly to help.

Work was not easy to find. I applied at every business, answered every newspaper ad, and when I finally got a shot at a cook's job, they told me I was over-qualified. Discouraged, I helped myself to Mom's Librium that she kept on hand since my father's death. Little did she know that a couple of days before, I had literally held a .22 pistol to my forehead. Right as I was ready to pull the trigger, I was interrupted by Mom and Genes' early return from fishing.

Sitting in the driveway, with the gun at my head, I heard their car approaching and just couldn't have my Mom find me that way. Despite the pain, I was in, the reality of her finding me that way, stopped me. Mom was genuinely concerned about me as she suspected that I was suicidal. An appointment was made with a shrink, and as usual I was horribly nervous.

"Is there some reason that you haven't taken off those black sunglasses?" the psychiatrist asked as I walked in.

"I never take my glasses off, unless I'm sleeping," I told him.

I sat down and spilled my guts about the acid trip, the years of violence, etc. He assured me that the acid had left my body within two days after I took it. He told me that the fear attacks and constant paranoia were all in my head. No kidding! That didn't help a whole lot, as I already knew that. He ended up prescribing a generic equivalent to Valium and sent me on my way.

Depression grew heavier and heavier, so I decided to move back to Fresno to good old Danny's house. At seventeen Danny had lost his brand-new wife in a car crash. Headed for Bass Lake, they had a head-on collision, and his wife was thrown from the car. She died in Danny's arms, leaving him with a 6-month-old daughter. Later, Danny turned his daughter over to his in-laws to raise. Never recovering from the loss, Danny became an alcoholic like me.

Danny learned the plastering trade from his father. Whenever Dan needed help, his father was always there. Danny was living with him when I hit town and his dad invited me to stay with them. Living in my car, and sometimes sleeping in his backyard, I hoped that I could go to work with them when they needed an extra hand.

Ironically, Dan's dad was actively working with Alcoholics Anonymous in Fresno. Often, he would let men who were trying to "dry out" stay with him until they got themselves together.

Work came to a total halt and for three weeks, no one called. Laying in the back yard drunk we would stumble to the store to buy more vodka. After three solid weeks I had alcohol poisoning and we had run out of booze and money. Danny and I soon got on each other's nerves and change was coming.

Doug, another childhood friend, dropped by Dan's and wanted me to go to Bass Lake with him. Doug had the money for booze, so off I went. We hitchhiked up there; and at the local store, right down from the Pines Bar we bought ourselves a gallon of wine. It was the 4th of July weekend and the bar right next to where we were sitting was full of Hells Angels.

Doug and I finished our gallon of wine and headed to the bar for more. We walked right in and sat down in the middle of all those bikers and started ordering straight shots of tequila. I minded my own business, but they threw Doug out on his ear. Doug went to jail after being chased by the sheriff.

Sitting literally in a gutter, outside of the bar, barefoot with a pair of jeans, a vest and not a dime, I had hit the bottom. No car, no friends, no home, and so ashamed of it all. The fear and paranoia would not stop, and I could not seem to help myself.

Up drove a car of some people I knew from Fresno, and they offered me a ride back to Fresno after they watched the Fourth of July fireworks display. I remember literally crawling into their back seat and hiding until they dropped me off back in town.

Something had to change. I headed for the town of Visalia and ended up at my younger sister Penny's house. Little Sis was in the middle of a painful separation, so I thought she didn't really mind me staying there.

8

Destiny and Diana

I landed a job at a restaurant called the Chinowith House, but my problem with the panic attacks, anxiety and fear was overwhelming. I remember I used to go to work after I was buzzed. My daily routine was to wake up, take some Valium or Librium, down two quarts of beer and then I was ready to deal with work. Arriving mid-day, I would hide a bottle of vodka by a tree outside the back door where employees took cigarette breaks. As the night wore on and the pressures of work got to me, I would slip outside for a sip.

My brother Pat was bartending at one of the finest restaurants in Visalia, named The Depot. Heading there after work, I would drink until Pat stopped pouring. One fateful night I sat drinking alone at the darkened end of the bar. I remember this very bubbly, energetic, little cocktail waitress that kept catching my attention. She was a cute, sexy little thing, with hardly anything on, because of the outfits they were supposed to wear.

Bouncing my way, this waitress said, "Hi there!" I just stared straight ahead and ignored her. "Your loss!" she said without hesitating and sped away.

My brother Pat asked, "What do you think of that little chick?" Pridefully, I said, "Oh, she's all right. A little dingy though."

Later that same night I was headed for Tulare, a little town eight miles away and asked Pat to "call that little chick over here."

Introducing us, Pat explained that I was his brother and needed a ride to Tulare. Diana was her name and shockingly she said "Sure, but we'll have to stop by my Mother's first so I can change."

When we got to her Mother's, the first thing she did to win my heart, or should I say craving, was to pour me a glass of wine. Then, on a beautiful stereo, she blasted my favorite group, The Temptations! Somehow, even with her parents out of town, we never made it any farther that night.

Seeing each other every day after that at her work, Diana, made a valiant effort to keep up with my drinking. One night against my brother Pat's wishes, I started drinking tequila, which usually made me crazy. "Fine!" said Diana and at that, downed straight shots of tequila with beer backs, one for one with me. She held her own until we stepped out of the bar into the cold night air. As the cold night air hit her, she did a classic fall, straight back into a flowerbed. I picked her up and headed for her mother's house, where I had been allowed to stay on the couch downstairs the night before. She sobered up enough on the way home to invite me up to her room.

I asked, "Are you crazy lady?"

"Oh, no," she assured me. "My mother sleeps across the hall and it's perfectly all right."

Well, with the life I had led before, I had met some weird moms, so what the heck? Drunk from tequila, we got undressed and passed out. The next thing I remember was staring into the face of a flashlight and a man's voice ordering me to get up and get dressed. Yelling at Diana to cover up I said, "What do you guys want?"

Dennis and Diana, the early years

The two huge policemen standing over the bed politely said, "This young lady's mother has called us, and you have to leave immediately."

To say that I was embarrassed would be an under-statement, but my shyness was overshadowed by my anger. I was furious. The next day when Diana called, my friend Kenny Ray answered the phone.

KR was a high school buddy of mine, whom I started hanging around with. He had literally fried himself on an acid trip but was the nicest guy you'd ever want to meet. He came over to Penny's every day and we would listen to oldies but goodies and drink anything we could get our hands on. I asked Kenny who it was.

"It's Diana."

"Tell that broad to go jump in a lake," I said.

"I can't Dennis; she's crying man. I mean she's beggin'."

After Kenny kept bugging me, I went to the phone. I was determined to never see her again, but when I heard her crying, my heart softened. "Come on over," I offered, as she told me that she had been kicked out and had told her Mom off. Then I mentioned a quart of beer would be nice.

Without missing a day, we continued seeing each other and spent every spare minute together. After a few weeks I decided to call things off. Picking Diana up from work I said, "There's something I've got to tell you."

"What?" she said smiling back at me.

"I can't see you anymore."

"What?" she screeched. "Why not?"

"It's not going to work because I'm really… really starting to like you and if I get burned by one more girl, I'm liable to kill somebody."

Not even batting an eye, she replied, "Is that all?" Are you nuts? You don't have to worry about me leaving you. You probably couldn't get rid of me."

"I'm dead serious," I shouted.

"SO AM I!" she said right back in my face.

No one had ever got in my face before. *She's just as crazy as I am*, I remember thinking. So, issue settled, we continued to spend every moment together that we could.

A short time later, Diana's parents left for a week to Hawaii and she was back on speaking terms with them and was living back at home. I believe now that her mom calling the cops was well within reason and after reconciling, her mother even joked about it.

"What a funny story to tell the grandkids someday if you end up together."

Totally against house rules, Diana invited me to stay there for a week this time. From the day we met I cannot remember spending one day or night apart; and we desperately clung to each other. My wife will relate the following part of my story, to you; and after reading it you'll understand why.

9

Violence

Diana:
Dennis was still drinking beer early in the day as a rule to calm his nerves; but I had talked him out of needing Librium daily. One sunny August morning I had no idea what was about to occur. The birds were singing a little tune out the dining room window and it promised to be another hot summer day.

Looking out over the pool in the back yard the wonderful aroma of freshly cooking bacon seemed to promise a great day. Walking towards the stove to finish making breakfast, I was totally shocked when Dennis said, "Go get me a bottle of vodka." He laughed like it was no big thing and laughing back I said "No way! You don't need that this early in the morning."

Dennis laughed again and said, "Oh, come on. I won't drink it till tonight."

"Good," I replied. "I'll get you some tonight then!"

This was totally blowing my mind because he had appeared to be doing much better. Dennis was stone sober. He hadn't had Librium for around a week and nothing to drink since dinner the night before. But he persisted.

"No, Dennis" I kept saying.

I was honestly getting worried. I cared for this guy and I started realizing he really had deep problems. As I refused to go buy vodka, even though he kept laughing, I sensed he was getting angrier and angrier. Suddenly, the next thing I knew, Dennis was threatening to kill me, but this was more than that.

Before meeting Dennis, I had met the most amazing woman. Lori was her name, and as I was being threatened, memories of what she had taught me sprang up inside.

"Jesus!" I screamed out to God.

I was not touching Dennis and I'll never forget. It seemed like something out of the "Exorcist" when his body was thrown back against the couch at the sound of that name. He was three feet from the couch and was thrown back on his rear. His eyes rolled and looked glazed and the next words he said were, "What's going on?" Then his eyes got intense with hatred and from his mouth I heard a voice that was not his say, *"I hate you and I'm going to kill you."*

If you have ever looked into the eyes of a murdering demon, you will never forget it.

"JESUS!" I screamed each time he tried to get from the couch to come near me. It was as if someone repeatedly came between us; and to this day I'm convinced that angels were intervening. Running to the phone, I dialed the phone number that sprang up in my mind. Just as I got through and spoke.

"Lori—help!" Dennis slammed down the receiver. But through the repeated calls, Lori got across the words,

"Bring him over here."

Several times Dennis tried to grab the phone and ended up back on the couch when I cried out that name. His eyes would roll and first this demon spirit would say that it hated me and then Dennis would be weeping and asking, "What just happened?"

Every time this spirit would manifest, Dennis would blank. Telling Dennis that I was going to take him for some help, we headed towards the back door.

Walking past an open dishwasher full of clean dishes, I had my back to Dennis. DANGER I heard a small inner voice say and as I whirled around, I saw, poised in the air, a butcher knife that had just reached the top of its assent. "Jesus" I shouted; and Dennis' wrist literally went limp and he dropped the knife. Making it out the door, down the steps, and into the car, I was amazed at what was happening.

In the car, headed for the Travelodge Motel where the woman named Lori worked, that still small voice urgently let me know that Dennis was going to try to grab the steering wheel, so commanding his arm to be still in that name, I watched as his hand went back to his lap. The rest of the short ride was uneventful.

As we arrived at the motel I said, "Come on in, just for a minute."

"I'll wait in the car," Dennis offered.

"No," I said, "You really must meet this lady".

Walking into the manager's apartment, Dennis' eyes darted around the room. Dennis later told me he couldn't believe his good fortune. A man named Reed, who was an old drinking buddy of his, sat on the couch grinning away at him. Good old Reed will have some booze, and he'll offer me a drink, Dennis thought.

"Reed, what's up?" Dennis asked.

"Hey, Dennis," Reed replied. Dennis didn't know that Reeds' life had changed, and he was no longer the town drunk.

"Sit down and visit awhile," Reed invited.

Dennis was no sooner on the couch than Lori smiled and said, " I hear you've been having a little trouble honey?" Suddenly this thing in Dennis glared at Lori.

"I'm going to kill everyone in the room." This voice growled.

Lori recognized an old foe and gently but firmly laying her hands-on Dennis stomach and forehead declared, "Oh no you're not!"

"You come out of him, you murdering demon, and I mean NOW! In Jesus' name, you've got to go!"

From deep within, this thing started to scream. It didn't give a lot of screams, just one long, long scream that built in volume and you could hear the wail go across the room and out of the door of the apartment. Sitting completely limp in an air-conditioned apartment, Dennis' clothes were so wet that you could have wrung them out. Dennis had literally slid onto his knees off the edge of the couch in pure exhaustion.

Lori said, "Honey, what you need is Jesus."

I will never forget, the humble broken man, who stared at Lori, and literally said, "I don't even know what you mean, but if he will help me YES!"

After praying with Lori, Dennis smiled, and looked absolutely stunned. The journey would take a lifetime, but something major had happened.

10

Going to the Chapel

Dennis:

Several mornings later at the motel, while lying on the bed, I shouted "Hey, Diana!" to where she was showering. "They're not going to let us stay here forever. We need to find some place to live." Answering from the bathroom, Diana replied, "Well, I don't believe in living together. If I love you enough to share the same house and bed, I love you enough to marry you."

Thinking, I paused for a minute.

"Well, let's get married!" I yelled back.

Calling out of the bathroom, Diana said, "Don't tease me about something like that. I really love you."

Try to remember that this is the same woman that had almost been murdered by me less than three days before.

"Who's teasing?" I asked. "Where do you go for something like that?"

Charging into the room Diana leapt on top of the bed while whooping and choking me with hugs.

"We could go to Reno. Today!" she said without hesitation.

That's what I like about my wife. She never lets a golden opportunity pass! A few weeks was all that we had known each other, but deep inside we really believed we couldn't do without one another.

After packing our things up, we thanked Reed and Lori, informed them of our plans, and headed for Diana's mother's house to tell her.

We had returned to clean the house before they got back from Hawaii, but had chosen to stay at the motel, so we could be together. Not owning a car, a decent pair of pants, shoes, or a shirt, I had a few minor details to take care of.

First, I borrowed a pair of black Angel Flight pants and matching shoes from my brother, Pat, and then arriving at Diana's house we told her mom. Ivan, Diana's father, was down in Los Angeles, so we asked Dorothy if we could borrow the car. I'm sure she wondered what planet we flew in from, asking her for my future father-in-law's car and a shirt. So many people wait to get married until they have the perfect set-up, and here we were with nothing but ourselves and sixty dollars and... going to elope. Terribly romantic if you think about it.

I had never had the pleasure of meeting Ivan yet; and he just happened to call before we took off.

"Hello, Ivan? Nice to meet you. May I borrow your car and have your daughter?"

Ivan stayed perfectly calm and replied, "What can I say? Just love her and take good care of her!"

As we got in the car, Diana's mom looked at her and said, "Honey, are you sure?"

"Yes, Mom." was the reply.

Driving away, I couldn't help but notice that Dorothy looked concerned. I wondered what she would have thought had she known about the events of the last week.

Boy, was I nervous and about one hour out of Reno. We both were so tired, neither of us could drive, so we pulled into a motel to spend the night. The sun rose early and so did I. Fear was really attacking my mind. Sensing it, Diana said,

"Don't do anything you are not sure of."

"Hey, I can get out of it as easy as I got in" I laughed.

Fears of so many things flooded my mind, and I admitted, I didn't love myself, and I sure didn't know how to love someone else.

Diana patiently listened and shared that all she knew, is she believed we were supposed to be together in her heart of hearts.

Discussion settled, off we headed to find a place to get married. At a gas station outside of Reno, Diana picked up a brochure advertising the "Starlight Wedding Chapel." The pamphlet offered five dollars off the ceremony, free parking, dressing rooms, five dollars' worth of gambling tokens, complimentary champagne, and a gift. If that didn't grab you, the chapel was directly across the street from where we had to get our license.

Later, Diana told me she got the pamphlet out of a holder that was sitting on the back of the toilet. Classy!

Applying for the license went smoothly, except for the fact that I had left my identification in the car. The lady filling out the legal papers said, "Oh, no problem. You don't need any." Right! We returned to the car to find a parking ticket on the windshield, which I promptly threw on the ground. After all, we weren't from here and it was stupid. I really didn't care.

Walking into the actual wedding chapel felt like a tour of Universal Studios and it had all the appeal of a fake television set. No one was at the desk and we didn't know whether to pick up the phone sitting there or what. A few minutes later this lady appeared out of nowhere. Kindly, she took all the information and asked us if we wanted wedding rings. "Definitely," Diana answered. The lady continued to fill out our paperwork and then ushered us into a couple of dressing rooms. Excitedly, Diana and I talked and joked back and forth while we changed. I stepped out of the dressing room and spotted the man who was to marry us. Poring over a copy of the National Enquirer, he had all the makings of a wax dummy. I mean this guy was loo-loo city. He didn't bother to look up, so I headed up front where Diana was waiting.

Positioning us at the entrance of the chapel, the secretary bellowed to the nameless man in the back room, "Ready?" As the "preacher" walked to the alter, this woman galloped through the front office, around back past the dressing rooms, behind the chapel, and plopped onto a piano bench where she banged out the wedding march. Diana and I were halfway down the aisle by the time she started playing.

"Do you have the rings?" The preacher asked discretely.

"No!" (I figured they would take care of that.)

"Stop!" yelled the preacher back to his helper.

Cloppity, clop, clop, we heard her heels clicking all the way as she literally galloped back up front. Escorting us out of the chapel, we followed her to a display case, picked out the rings, and paid for them; nothing like a business transaction to break the mood. Twenty dollars for both seemed quite the deal. 10K gold plated tin, or nickel.

Leading us back to the chapel entrance, we enjoyed a repeat performance, as our witness, and secretary / cashier, dashed madly back across the office, around the back past the dressing rooms, behind the chapel and simultaneously we heard the plop of her butt hitting the piano bench as her fingers started playing the wedding march. Again, we were nearly all the way to the altar before she began to play.

As the preacher spoke to us, I looked at Diana and noticed she was on the verge of a laughing fit, right then and there. This man's voice never changed in volume, tone, or inflection during the whole ceremony, and sounded suspiciously like a recording. All that was left to do was to concentrate on the words and the fact that I knew these vows were between Diana, God, and me. How the preacher sounded didn't matter.

Well, we had done it! I had made a huge step and it didn't even hurt. After gambling our nickels, we headed out of town to pick up our free champagne and gift. With 8 ounces of champagne and a plastic pair of salt and peppershakers that said, "South Lake Tahoe," we headed out. Destination: Anderson, California to tell my mother.

Arriving at the same mobile on the Sacramento River where I had almost blown my brains out, here I was tapping on the door to introduce my new wife.

"Hi, Mom! Meet your new daughter in-law."

Mom laughed and said, "Oh, sure! That'll be the day."

Diana said seriously, "Mom, look at my ring!"

Mother replied, "Oh, that ring could have come from Woolworth's for all I know."

Mother finally picked up that it was real and realized that Diana was her new daughter in-law. "Oh, you guys, you crazy kids!" Hugging us, she gave us hearty congratulations. Since it was around four in the afternoon, "Pop" was due home soon.

After dinner, Diana and I played poker with Mom and Gene and literally won our gas money home. Mom and Diana headed to bed leaving Gene with me to visit. Gene proceeded to tell me that everything I had experienced wasn't real. Gene meant well, but he wasn't there.

I guess we really got carried away and I had forgotten that I had just gotten married. I tried to make up for it when I got to bed. Diana was quite upset and to this day she teases me about it.

11

Under the Tree

As we drove home to Visalia the next morning, we went straight to Penny's to tell her we were married. We were so excited to get back home, plus we both had to work the very next day. We had fooled my sister Penny before we left and asked her for sixty dollars to go gambling with.

Hearing I was married she jumped for joy as she thought I would never settle down, and I was glad to see her happiness, as later she admitted she thought Diana was just another girlfriend. Penny lived in a little two-bedroom house on the north side with her children. "Not much room, but you're welcome to it," she offered.

It was summertime and for about a week Diana and I stayed out under a big tree in Penny's front yard. We didn't mind the lawn; we were in love! I've always enjoyed telling people that we started out underneath a tree. We would curl up under a blanket, try not to leave any left-over food around to attract any ants, and snuggled as if this were normal.

Ivan and Dorothy had forgiven us all the craziness, and even threw us quite a wedding reception at their house. My new in-laws had offered us quite a gift. Diana and I could either take a honeymoon to Hawaii or have cash and use the money to rent an apartment. Probably for the first time since we met, we took the adult choice and started looking for an apartment right away.

Locating a tiny apartment, we were ready to set up house. There was just enough room in the one small bedroom to fit a double bed, which you had to sit on to use the closet. The kitchen was very handy, as you could reach the fridge, sink, stove, and table without moving one step. We used cardboard boxes set upside down for end tables and with one sofa, chair, and a TV, we had home sweet home.

For transportation we had bought Penny's old, white Ford Falcon. After Pat and I switched the gearshift to the floor, it had only two gears. Running around town with second and third only, you had to be incredibly careful which way you parked, as it had no reverse.

Meanwhile, a patron of my brother's bar had started a landscaping company and offered to let me work for him and trying yet another job, I wanted to help financially any way I could. Beginning our new life together, we continued to drink heavily, and we argued a lot the first year, although regardless of the issue, the alcohol didn't help.

Diana spent several months making me the most amazing food, and finally sharing how she was bored started looking for a job. Landing a job as assistant manager of a lady's apparel shop seemed to meet the need. With extra money coming in we searched for a new place to live, as we had been invited to leave our little apartment. Coincidentally, we discovered the two-bedroom house across the street from my sister Penny's was up for rent.

We rented that house for $350 a month, $200 cheaper than the going rate. What a blessing it was.

12

Job to Job

My older brother, Jack, was looking for a business to get into so I suggested landscaping. I had not received a raise in months and when I asked for one my boss just laughed. Laughing back, I spat on his shoe and walked off the job.

My oldest brother Jack thought landscaping sounded good, and I assured him that I could teach him what I had learned in the time I had been landscaping. Jack moved to Visalia and together we formed a landscaping company. We had a good time at first, but then more problems arose.

While I was still landscaping with Jack, Diana started work as a teachers' aide at a school called Riverbend. This school catered to the special needs of the developmentally disabled. I had a nephew named David with Down's Syndrome whom I was crazy about, so I was happy for her and the job she was doing.

Yet again, life, and injury, unemployment, and heavy drinking added up after hurting my knee right before Christmas. After a cold, hard winter, we found ourselves applying for food stamps the day after Christmas. A one pound half empty sack of flour was literally what was in the refrigerator when we decided we needed help. Sitting down, we realized that Diana's income alone was not enough, and my knee was having a heck of a time healing.

Diana believed God was knocking on our door; and she was beginning to listen. I have got to tell you it must have been hell on her to motivate me. Between my stubbornness and drinking, I was a bear when not working. Getting a local newspaper, we started searching the help wanted ads. Diana had mentioned seeing an ad three weeks before about someone needing live-in house-parents.

At the time, I said, "You've got to be kidding." Now, this same ad was back in the paper.

"What would you think about working with handicapped folks?" Diana asked. The ad says, "House-parents needed to live in and care for six children. Some yard-work also included in the job description." The timing of this new ad was incredible.

After the first time Diana saw the ad, I had taken a job at what was known as Sin City, some sleazy apartments that really needed to be torn down. Along with that job came an apartment. This was going to help meet the bills, so we had already given Bernice, our current landlady, notice. We did not have any money for rent and only had ten days until we had to be out of our house. Two days of working for those apartments I discovered that they didn't have tools and expected me to be a mechanic. Calling Diana, I told her, I can't work here but we won't have an apartment. Diana was furious how they had lied to me, and said, "I'll pick you up right now."

Here it was eight days until we had to be moved, with no job, no place to live, and no money. Combing the want ads in the local paper, Diana couldn't believe the same ad for house parents was now back in. I didn't know anything about taking care of kids, but the yard work looked up my alley, so I told Diana to call the number.

A lady named Mary Jo answered the phone and after hearing of Diana's experience at the school for handicapped, she said to come for an interview. Pulling up in front of a ranch-style, country home we almost fainted. The main home was huge with a pool, a beautiful yard, and next door was a brand-new triple wide mobile home.

During the interview, we discovered the ad had been in three weeks before, but someone had been hired. That person was to start days before and never showed up. Mary Jo had literally placed the ad back in the paper the day I quit "Sin City." Another strange thing was that no one else had called but us, and after offering us the job Mary Jo told us to go out back by the pool to discuss it. While we were deciding four or five calls came in, asking for the job.

I asked Diana what she thought. "I don't know, this one's your decision," she replied. The offer was six hundred dollars a month, plus room and board. The mobile home was like a mansion after where we were living.

"What do you think?" asked Diana.

"You kidding? I know the answer. You're telling me someone is offering us money, food, and a place to live.... just to love these folks. Feed them, dress them, and bath them... all the things they cannot do for themselves? If I could, I would do it for free."

Driving home Diana told me she wanted to give all our belongings to a local charity that helped the poor. The new mobile was furnished down to dishes, and it didn't seem like anything else could be right.

Excitement was what I felt, and I will always remember the day we moved in. Our clothes, some plants, and a few personal belongings were all we had kept. Everything fit in the back of the old, 1964 short bed step side Chevy truck we were now driving. We wanted to get familiar with our newly adopted family: three girls and three boys, Michael, Richard, James, Griselda, Laura, and Kami.

Oh, did we do some growing up in those years. We absolutely fell in love with our new family and God knows we loved them just like our own. No one will ever know the precious memories they have given us. Sadly though, I found myself drinking more than ever. It was easy to get away with it, as we had a job that was at home.

Diana was there so if I needed to anesthetize a little, I knew she never drank while working, so I felt secure. This was a high-pressure job, and instead of joining in with my drinking, she was growing up and wasn't joining in.

One night, I had been in Visalia at the bar where my brother Pat worked. On the way home, once again, my life was almost taken. I was driving our light blue Volkswagen when another car being driven by a member of the Mongols biker gang ran into me. All I remember was spinning around. When the car stopped, I got out and saw everything from the car door back totaled.

Diana told me later that at the time of the accident she had felt a great weight and started praying for me. The biker and I were drunk, and words flew about whose fault it was. At any rate, this biker went to a phone and called a group of his friends to come get him as his vehicle wouldn't run either. A short time later a group of his friends showed up in a truck wearing their colors and it was obvious they were not happy.

Drunk, I jumped in one guy's face and demanded a cigarette. Somehow, rather than getting beat up I wrangled a ride home. Furious about the whole incident I stormed into the house and grabbed an old .22 pistol of my Dad's and raced out the back door. I blamed the other guy, even though I had turned in front of him.

"What are you doing with that gun? What's happening?" Diana frantically gasped. I ignored her and started to aim at the pickup, but I had changed. Despite being drunk, I aimed at the ground and shot one round into the dirt, then went back inside.

The next day I received a call from the guy threatening to blow me away, and the mobile home along with it. The next night was so foggy you couldn't even see ten feet. Sitting in our living room, Diana and I heard the roar of God knows how many bikers and thank God even though they had been there the night before, somehow, they couldn't seem to find the place. I never heard from the guy again and our insurance company handled all the details.

Not long after that incident, Mary Jo was getting ready to replace us with her husband, so our social worker suggested we open our own home. He was impressed with the progress our folks had made, and for the record, had even written a letter recommending us to the head of the Regional Center, the agency who placed and monitored the clients.

We thought this was a great idea, as Diana was now pregnant, and we knew we would need a bigger place.

13

First Business and First Baby

Remember how I related to you how a panel of psychologists and psychiatrists had diagnosed me as paranoid and in need of a psych ward? Well, this time I had to go in front of a group of professionals that included doctors, nurses, social workers, program directors, etc. This group not only found us to be totally suited for the job and within three months of opening our own home had placed three clients with us.

Now living in the quaint little town of Porterville, CA, the regional center placed two of the girls from Mary Jo's in our new care home, so it was like old home week. Casey was the name of a beautiful collie that perfectly fit the little doghouse and fenced back yard of our new home. Our love nest was pale yellow with white trim. Two big bedrooms, a nursery, a living room with a brick fireplace and a gorgeous kitchen overlooking the dining room completed the house.

With Diana due, we were excited about the new baby, and I was mainly drinking beer, trying to control my dependency on alcohol.

"Let's go watch Randy (our nephew) play basketball." I said one weekend.

"Sure! And since it's forty miles to Visalia, I think I'll take my suitcase just in case," Diana said.

She looked at the main event of child birth more like going to spend the night at a girlfriend's house. Since she was three weeks from the due date, I thought she was crazy. Racing all over Visalia, looking for the right location of Randy's game, Diana and I kidded about the amount of railroad tracks we had crossed. Finally, walking into the local YMCA, we spotted Randy dribbling the ball down the court. We had just found a great spot to watch the game when Diana whispered,

"Uh oh, its happening, we need to go to my mother's."

"Go to your mother's?!!! Call a doctor!" I said.

"That's what I mean, I'll call him from Mother's," replied Diana.

Diana and I had been too busy for childbirth classes and her doctor assured her it would be ok. At Dorothy and Ivan's, we got the word to go on to the hospital. Checking Diana in, while she sang, "Let's get physical," we were informed we would have to take who ever was on call.

After waiting and waiting, I said, "Where is this guy?" Meantime, a rude nurse greeted us and for the next seven hours she complained constantly about missing a break and not getting a chance to stuff her face. Never having given birth herself, her maternal instincts equaled that of a tarantula's.

Sitting on the bed, I said, "Oh, no! Look Diana! If that man coming this way is the doctor, we're outta here!"

This guy looked like the nutty professor. An old, faded T-shirt hung on him, his hair looked like it had never been combed and to top off the spectacle, he was in his stocking feet. This man walked, to my horror, directly into our room and without introducing himself said,

"We're going to induce labor! It looks bad! We really could have trouble ahead. You've lost water and if the baby isn't here by midnight, we'll have to take the baby by C-section." The way he stated this, it sounded more like an offense to the body, not a helpful medical technique. Turning and walking out the door, he left.

After 14 hours of terrifying, hard, hard, labor by Diana, I felt like I had birthed the baby myself. But, oh, what a baby! Being three weeks premature, he weighed only six pounds seven ounces. Diana and I had picked out the name Isaac, which means laughter. Bringing brand new baby Isaac home on her birthday, Diana felt like he was the perfect present.

With two foster children and one baby, our busy lives picked up even more. Soon a third girl was placed with us, followed by yet another call from our social worker. "Would you accept placement of Richard to your home?" Oh, Diana and I jumped for joy. He was a little boy we had in our home at Mary Jo's. When we first met, he weighed 43 pounds and was 55 inches tall and was extremely sick. Diana called him her "baby bird," and nursed him back to health. With a special diet, but mainly love, within two months he weighed 75 pounds. Richard had also learned the words "baby" and "mama."

The only way to accept Richard was to have a bigger home. In one week, we had located and decided to buy a fellow care provider's home. The day we were to sign the paperwork, a licensing official put a halt to our plans. Another licensed care home was on the same street and we were told two on the same street were not allowed. We were disappointed, although we had not been crazy about the location of the house. It overlooked a drive-in that played cheap movies and worse, horror films.

14

Terra Bella

Looking in the paper the next morning, we decided to drive out and look at a house that was listed. "How much is it?" I asked Diana.

"Only $90,000" she replied.

I about fainted! We were barely making it; and we didn't have an extra dime. The only way we were going to get the first house was for the owner to carry the paperwork.

"Come on," Diana said.

Sure, I thought. Sure. My wife is the most optimistic woman in the world, and at that time I was the worst pessimist. Driving six miles to a little town called Terra Bella, we drove to the address and couldn't believe what we saw. The structure of the old country home looked okay. But what a mess!

The front porch door was wedged open with all kinds of junk, including an old washer. Weeds stood high at various places on the acre. The house was a faded olive green, there was an ugly redwood-stained fence running down both sides of a pool, and the fence wasn't connected at either end.

"I wouldn't give these people eighty dollars for this place," I told Diana.

"There must be a reason they're asking so much. Let's look inside." Diana said. "She's blind." I thought but I knew what she was thinking. We had always fixed up any rental we had been in, where they needed it.

Once on the porch, I saw a different story. A massive door with beveled glass led the way into an open living room with a cathedral ceiling overlooked by a loft. To my left was the largest fireplace I had ever seen. It spanned the main wall through the whole house and was made of massive mountain rocks. The fireplace mantel was literally a full slice out of a whole tree.

The home was 2000 square feet with four big bedrooms, all leading off from the main living room hacienda-style. Besides two extra-large bathrooms, there was a kitchen complete with pantry. But the big eye-catcher was a huge chandelier with a matching mini chandelier at the other end of the living room. As we passed a window box off the kitchen and headed out the back door a twenty by forty-foot swimming pool greeted us.

Diana's first words were, "This is it! This is the place!"

Now I knew she was nuts. We didn't have a quarter. As we were leaving, the realtor showed up. Her name was Alice. She was a real cutie and reminded us of Lois Lane from the Superman comic books. Alice was headed out of town so she asked if we could come to her office later? Well, my wife, Little Miss Optimist blurted out, "Sure. What time?" before I had a chance to protest. Later that day we went to Alice's office. The first thing Alice said was, "Kids, how much have you got?"

We said, "Money?"

She said "Yeah. You gotta have money to buy a house."

"God will take care of the money, let's just take care of the paperwork." Diana blurted out. She had greater faith than I did.

Alice to my surprise said, "Okay. Let's see what we can do. Are you a veteran?"

"Yes. I am." I mumbled.

"Have you ever used your Cal-Vet loan?" Alice asked hopefully?

"No." I said.

"Good, the guy that owns this house is a veteran, and he is trying to switch his loan to another house but has to have someone else take over this house, who is a veteran."

"Alright," we said. First hurdle passed!

"Do you have any assets to borrow on?" Alice inquired.

"What's an asset?" we joked. We had only been married three and a half years since starting out underneath Penny's tree.

"Do you have any relatives that could loan you some money?" Alice retorted.

"Maybe a little. How much do we need down?" Diana asked.

"Oh, if we offer $84,000, about $8500, just 10% down" Alice said as a matter of fact.

"Great." Diana said.

"Great, you say?" I silently thought.

Suddenly Reed my old golfing buddy came to mind. If nothing else, Reed could give us some good business advice. Mentioning Reed to the realtor I decided to head over to Tortilla Flats, the restaurant Reed and Lori were running.

Before we left, Alice said, "Hey, by the way, I need some money."

"How much?" Diana asked.

"Just $500. That will hold the house so no one can buy the house out from under you. You know. To put it into escrow" Alice said.

"No problem," said Diana. To my shock, she whipped out our checkbook and wrote a hot check for $500. Sure, I liked the house, but I didn't know if this was faith or lunacy! Getting outside she said, "Didn't you hear her? This check won't be cashed until we have a deal, but I'll see if Mom and Dad can lend us this for a week until our paycheck comes in, if that will make you feel better."

Arriving at the Flats, Reed not only gave us legal advice, but now we were much wealthier on paper. Our next move was to be approved by Cal-Vet. We were turned down, flat. No explanation. After many conversations and getting more paperwork, Cal-Vet gave the go ahead. Finally, there was the problem of $2,000. To get the placement of Richard, we had to get into a house right away.

My brother lent us $2,000; and the owner of the house said, "Sure, I'll rent to you until Cal-Vet closes escrow." Here within a month of the initial call from our worker, Diana, and I, found ourselves with a mansion when we didn't have an extra dime.

Now there was only one small final detail: $6,000 for the rest of the down when Cal-Vet was ready to close. Diana had no doubt it would work out and I was beginning to think it was a possibility. Everything was ready for the big move, except manpower. Packing, Diana took care to pack everything like a professional. To add to the chaos, we had received yet another female client on a temporary basis, just in time for the move.

Renting the U-Haul, I drove back to Conley St, wondering where time had gone. Arriving home, Diana and I packed the whole truck ourselves, except for the heaviest things. On moving morning my brother Pat showed up and was able to donate a few hours, but had a time limit as he had to work that day. Isaac was three months old by now; and with four of our special kids, we had our hands full.

The first trip wasn't too eventful, other than the new little girl who tried to kick the windows out of the moving van the whole time. The social worker had warned us she had behavioral problems. Diana had the baby and the other three girls in the Volkswagen with her as we went back and forth on the six-mile trip between the two houses.

After Pat left, Diana and I headed back to the house. It wasn't the 110-degree weather or having the windshield of the truck I was driving constantly kicked that bothered me, but moving the final piece of furniture, our king-size waterbed almost did us in. Time was running out and so was our energy. Between changing pampers on the adult kids (they were not toilet trained), Diana would breast feed the baby and try to help me. The last little bit of water wouldn't drain from the bed, so we physically drug it through the house onto the front lawn where it finished draining. Now all that was left was the frame of the waterbed, and we only had the rental truck for another forty five minutes. I was sick when I discovered the screws wouldn't come out by hand as they had used a power drill to put them in.

I had forgotten that Diana didn't have the strength of a man. As we wrestled the giant frame out of the bedroom and down the hallway, we had to stop at least ten times.

Diana was finally in tears and yelled, "Can't you find someone to help?"

I pointed out that we didn't have one neighbor on the block less than seventy five years old. As Diana sat on the front porch crying, I gave her some of her own medicine. "You just ask God for the strength, cause you're the one He picked to help me move."

Diana cried harder as she knew I was right. Standing up, she let out a karate yell and lifted that thing a final time and got it onto the truck lift. Now laughing, we gazed at the five kids hanging out the U-Haul and the Volkswagen. They were all screaming their heads off. Hungry and thirsty, it felt more like 150 degrees than 110.

Ready to go now, I gave the command, "Follow me, Diana!" Off we went to our new home in Terra Bella. By the time we unloaded the final things, the living room was full of our belongings. Nothing was put away. After returning the U-Haul, I bought Chinese food, and back home in our new house we literally sat in the middle of furniture, boxes, mattresses, you name it, and ate our food.

We were so tired we fell asleep that night, right in the middle of the whole mess. The next morning, we both just sat and stared. What a long way we were from under my sisters' tree on Divisadero Street.

15

Changes

Our lives were slowly but surely changing. By now we had been married over four years, and I was realizing my fuse was way to short and I carried so much stress. Every day little things drove me crazy, and to not act out and end up in jail, I learned to walk away, rather than explode with most others except, my wife.

As time seemed to fly, we received great news. Isaac had passed his first birthday and soon it was confirmed Diana was pregnant again. Between day programs, social workers, parents visiting, bible studies, and visiting relatives, life was absolutely rushing by.

Unlike our Isaac who was born three weeks, early, our next baby, decided he did not want to leave the nest. Three months of false labor and several weeks past our due date, things were starting to get even more crazy.

Back and forth, back, and forth, we would drive the forty-minute drive from our home to the town our doctor was in. Diana and I would visit her grandmother Sarah, and they would play cards, while I would watch tv. Then when the false labor would ease off, we would head back home to Terra Bella.

Grandma Sarah, suggested Diana should drink beer and eat pizza to get things going. Ahhhh, such is the wisdom of the old days. We did and then driving all the way home, we wondered if this baby would ever come.

After changing the folks, getting everyone settled and kissing Isaac goodnight Diana lumbered up the steep stairs to our loft. Following her, I think I was asleep in minutes after the pizza and beer.

Being shaken awake I heard Diana say,

"Get up, this is it."

"No more false alarms," I mumbled.

"Dennis, this is it," Diana snapped.

"Oh, gosh, hurry, HURRY!" I said.

Calling Nicole our relief worker, we made the long drive to the hospital in Visalia and at two o'clock in the morning our beautiful middle son Isaiah joined our family and now with our Isaac, we had a family of four, six folks, a collie, a cockapoo, and more cats than you can count.

Receiving two more folks as full time placements and a higher income, I decided it was time for my life's dream, so motorcycle shopping I went. After getting an advanced case of "Harleyitis" I came home and announced it was time for me to have a Harley! I even tried to buy Diana a matching one, but she would have no part of it.

Taking Diana with me, I purchased a brand new 1984 low-rider. Leather saddlebags, a 36" sissy bar and two matching helmets completed the purchase. The color was deep purple, with gunmetal gray accents. Soon I was living a fantasy that nearly took my life.

Within a few weeks I would wait until out of sight of our home, then take off my helmet and add black knuckle motorcycle gloves. The dark sunglasses were back on for the first time in years. I usually rode alone and would head to the mountains with my favorite bottle of vodka. I'd drink till I passed out, sleep for most the day, then head home late at night. As the summer headed to a close, I was drinking heavier and heavier. The conviction of what I was doing drove me crazy because I was trying to hide the drinking from my wife.

On our fifth wedding anniversary, I was five hours late to meet her at the Holiday Inn. She had arranged for a sitter for the clients and dropped the kids with a relative and was happily awaiting my arrival at our motel rendezvous wondering what I was going to surprise her with.

Well surprised she was when after I stopped at the bar downstairs, I called the room where she was waiting, to set her straight. "I'll be up in a bit," I said and downed a few more for courage to face her in my condition.

Looking for a fight, I was shocked when Diana greeted me at the door and invited me in, and headed to a little setting area in the motel room, to hear what I had to say.

"I'm tired of trying to hide my drinking and smoking from you all the time," Plopping down at the table I lit a cigarette, blew smoke right in her face and said, "If you don't want me to drink or smoke in the house, I'll find somewhere else to do it." She stared at me, and after refusing to join in my trying to self-destruct, she calmly replied.

"I know you've been trying to hide all these things, but don't do it for my sake. I never asked you to hide anything. I love you. You're having some battles and I'm here to help."

You know it's extremely hard to fight unconditional love. I did not understand where she was getting the strength to love me when I couldn't love myself.

A few days later I was driving my Harley from a bar in Visalia toward home. Filled with rage, I remember just flat burying the needle in the speedometer. When I got home all the lights were out and I slumped down on the fireplace hearth. I remember saying, "What are you doing to yourself?"

A picture of my two precious boys passed before my eyes and a voice said, "You are going to die if you continue the way you are going!" I told Diana the next day what had happened and asked her to sell my bike. I told her my boys were more important to me than any motorcycle. I loved my family so much and felt great about my decision. She hadn't said a word and was so happy.

"Since I'm selling my bike, I'll trade it in on a new pickup." I demanded.

The pickup I chose was a cream colored 1984 Chevy Stepside pickup, the truck I'd wanted my whole life. Yet even all these new things could not get rid of the pain that still lingered after all these years. One night I came home so drunk I have no idea how I got home. Black outs were happening more and more, and I knew I just could not keep living this way.

I remember many different feelings and emotions flooded through me. Yelling and screaming, I stumbled around the living room, and blamed everyone else, for what I was doing. "I've tried all this religious garbage," I shouted. I was breaking everything in sight, including the glass shades covering the bulbs of the chandeliers.

Grabbing a large wooden framed picture of Jesus that sat on the mantle over our fireplace I angrily smashed it to pieces on the rocks and iron. "If you're real, why haven't you taken this alcohol and fear from me?" I challenged. In between bellowing questions, my fists would smash against the thick wrought iron gates to the fireplace. Blood was spattered everywhere and once again I was screaming out for help the only way I knew how, violently.

Diana had run the kids out of the living room when I had started screaming and tried to cover their little ears.

My knuckles shattered, blood and glass everywhere, I knew what I had to do.

Stumbling outside, I went to where my vodka bottle was hidden and poured it all out.

When I did, suddenly, I was sober. Exhausted I headed back in and slumped on the couch. Diana dressed my hands and cleaned the blood up then she brought out my two sons to me. Drained, I clung to them and fell asleep. For twenty-five years after that I never touched a drop of alcohol. I gave my sons the gift of a sober father.

One day during a potluck many adults were sitting around the pool and several were wading around the shallow end in the water. Playing with my son, Isaiah, I heard a wail from a child that had fallen. Leaping to his aid, I left Isaiah seated on a step with adults near him and said keep an eye on him. The baby that had fallen on the wooden deck was crying hard, so I walked him for nearly five minutes around the edges of the property.

Coming back, I spotted Isaiah, face down and motionless in the middle of the pool. Screaming, I dropped the child I had been holding, and raced to the pool. Diving in I grabbed Isaiah and drug him to the edge of the pool. Diana was at the store; and there I was staring at my son, who was lifeless. I raced around our acre screaming "Heal my baby! Heal my baby!"

Thoughts came immediately taunting saying, "Your baby is going to be brain damaged just like the handicapped children you take care of." Shouting out "NO!" I was scared to death and as I paced and ran all over the property there was no response.

Seeing Diana driving up, I ran towards her screaming.

"Diana, Isaiah was in the pool!"

Jumping out of the truck Diana ran to me and literally jerked that baby from my arms and yelled his name.

"Isaiah!"

Instantly, Isaiah's eyes opened, and he said,

"Mom."

From grey, lifeless, to flesh colored and speaking, our son was back. Huddled in our front yard all we could do was cry and be grateful.

16

Trust

One day Diana said, "I believe changes are coming." All the folks had made monumental progress. Our folks had excelled in many areas, but for the last two years they had reached a plateau.

Diana was now pregnant with our third baby and we went to a convention for a time of rest and reflection. While there we realized how burnt out, we were from caring for so many folks twenty-four/seven. The folks we loved but between nonstop medical needs, licensing, day programs, meetings with schools, placement agencies, and relatives? We had hit a wall.

Arriving home, within a few days a call came asking us, if we would come to Oklahoma, to help a couple who wanted to help rehab homeless people and build a community on their property. The job included a home, and basics like food, and at the time it seemed like a great way to head a new direction.

The couple were relatives of dear friends and has some really big dreams. They owned apartments in the slums of Odessa, Texas and had bought an abandoned school, complete with many structures and acreage in Tecumseh, Oklahoma. Their vision was to create a safe place for addicts to come live and work while recovering and get them away from the streets of Odessa.

From the time that we were married, Diana and I seemed to meet and attract troubled people everywhere we went, and our hearts were to help in any way we could. Giving away most everything we owned to friends, we stuffed the rest into a twelve-foot U-Haul. A trailer hitch on the back towed our 1978 Audi that we had purchased for eight hundred dollars cash; and what a spectacle it was!

"Diana, grab the boys and let's not forget Goliath, our little cockapoo. Time to roll out!"

Here, I must share with you yet one more true story. Two years before we had bought Goliath from a local pet store. Born December 24th, weighing one pound, he was the cutest little thing you ever did see.

Two weeks after buying him from the pet store, with no warning, Goliath became ill. A veterinarian confirmed the worst. He was blind and had severe coccidia (A dog disease), his distended bloated stomach was ready to pop; and he could not walk. "Take him back to where you got him and maybe they'll give you a refund," was all the hope that was offered.

Doing just that, Diana and I dropped him off, trying to figure out what to say to our oldest son, Isaac. Heading home, Diana, with tears streaming down her face prayed for our little puppy; and Isaac offered a hearty AMEN!

Twenty-four hours later a surprised pet storeowner was on the phone. "I don't understand it," he said, "But your dog appears fine. I came into the store this morning, and he was wagging his tail, and seemed simply fine. He can see, his stomach is not bloated and he is actually perky. Come pick him up."

WOW! We did; and after a thorough inspection by the vet, Goliath was pronounced totally fine. It was comical how the vet seemed almost offended by the turn of events, as he could not explain it. So on top of being the cutest little thing on earth, Goliath has his own special story to endear him to our family.

Grabbing Goliath, we hopped into the front of the U-Haul, shut the door and waved goodbye to our special home. We were on our way with $2,300 in our pocket.

We were so excited and for the first time in years, we enjoyed time with just our little family. I'll never forget how beautiful the ride was. I remember one stop that we made at a Holiday Inn. On day two of our journey, we were in the middle of the Colorado Mountains.

Walking from the motel, we came across a little baseball field.

The grass was a deep, rich green and looked so lush. Taking a deep breath, Diana and I just laid on the grass, while the boys ran to their hearts content up and down the field. We could not believe how it felt like a thousand pounds dropped off our shoulders.

I guess we didn't realize how caring for six folks twenty-four seven, Bible studies of many people, and children, had taken a toll.

What a beautiful country we live in. Driving through Kansas with its never-ending wheat fields, we couldn't wait to see our good friend Mamma Lori. Yep, that's the same Lady who prayed for me at the Travelodge, was now the manager of a restaurant called The Branch.

It was connected to a beautiful motel called the Salina Inn in the town of Salina, Kansas. Lori graciously offered to have us as her guests for a few days of rest and relaxation before we continued to Oklahoma. Lori worked at the restaurant; and we tried to share all the wonderful things that happened in Terra Bella in a few short visits at the restaurant.

Anxious to see what the future held for us, we said our good-byes and once again headed down the road. We had called Paul and Maxine, the founders of the property we were headed for and they were excitedly expecting us, too. Rolling through Tecumseh, we followed directions to find the spot called Harjo. Driving through gorgeous woods with leaves just turning color, autumn warmly greeted us.

Spotting the dirt road that had been described to us over the phone, we turned left. Running up the road to greet us was this young woman, who was so excited she absolutely could not contain herself.

After introducing herself she led us up the hill to where the old school was, while explaining why she was extra bubbly that day. She and her husband had been without transportation and had no money to fix their broken car. At midnight, the night before, someone unknown had driven up the lane and in the dark, had left a car.

When Billy, Shirley's husband, checked the car out he discovered an envelope with their names on it. Inside was the title to the car showing Billy and Shirley as owners and a car lot receipt marked paid in full. Billy went so far as to go to the car lot to see if a well-meaning friend had done it, but never found out who had given it. They were elated.

Arriving on the school property, we headed for a small, white house on one corner of the property. Knocking at the door, I was greeted by Paul! Handshakes went to hugs and it was only moments until his wife, Maxine, arrived on the scene and welcomed us with Oklahoma fervor.

17

Trials and Tribulations

The mobile home we were to live in had not arrived yet, so our belongings were loaded into the gym up the hill. Paul and Maxine insisted that we take their house and they retired to a little trailer parked on the property. It was such a change from the chaos of Terra Bella and Diana, and I were still reveling in our newfound freedom.

We both showered our boys with attention, and thanked God for such a wonderful opportunity to enjoy our family. The mobile home arrived, and so did the rains and cold weather. Here I got my first experience at playing plumber. The mobile home that had arrived had virtually every pipe leaking from some point or other.

Not being familiar with copper plumbing, I had my work cut out for me. To this day my wife teases me about the red stains I got on all my clothes from that red Oklahoma clay. For two full weeks I fought plumbing, and now I think I could probably tackle plumbing a whole house by myself.

Maxine felt we should be based in Oklahoma about a year, yet there was turmoil in my spirit. After roofing parts of the gym, I shared with Diana that something was about to happen. "I don't believe I'm here to remodel buildings." Driving down the road after getting some things in town the next day, I was shocked with a strong feeling that we would not be there long.

Getting home I told Diana, who an hour later received a call from Maxine. "Honey, the couple in Texas has had personal problems and I'm afraid we'll need you to go down there soon. How soon? In a couple of days."

Two days away was Isaiah's second birthday, and the news Diana's grandmother, Sarah, had passed away. When I first met Diana, we traveled to where her grandma lived and visited for a few days. Grandma wouldn't go anywhere and had not been well. Her body had recovered, but she just had lost her sparkle.

I asked her a few questions, which led to hours of looking at pictures when she was a young girl. Transformed with memories, Sarah giggled and told wonderful stories. Wouldn't you know that the next day she agreed to go to a museum out of town, that had a plaque dedicated to her husband who had passed away.

Sarah ended up having the time of her life. From that time on she decided she still wanted more in life. I remember Diana telling me that Sarah had asked her "Is he the one?" Diana quickly replied, "Yes, Grandma."

Eating together at the huge school dining hall where we had cooked, ate potlucks, and fellowshipped with some sweet people, I ate some birthday cake and reflected on what had occurred in our six weeks in Oklahoma.

Leaving many things behind, we headed for Odessa, Texas early the next morning. Trailing Paul's long yellow Cadillac was a six-foot brown trailer, holding just bare necessities. Following in our Audi, the 14-hour drive seemed longer, due to our car being packed to the hilt. I remember Isaiah perched on top of a microwave, and Isaac was surrounded by pictures, plates, and stuffed animals.

"Bare necessities," my wife had said.

Pulling in at midnight, Diana and I were thrilled. The neighborhood and apartments weren't as bad as we had expected. It was a bad part of town, but we had envisioned thugs on our doorstep, with derelicts hanging out of every tree.

Walking into our sleeping place for the night, a reality of the needs sharply loomed in our faces. A gutted apartment with a filthy couch covered with cigarette burns greeted us, complete with pieces of half smoked joints left by transients. Too tired to care, I saw a mattress on the floor in one room, and to heat us that night was a gas stove a room away. Broken windows and a urine-stained toilet glared at us from the end of a tiny hallway. A single light bulb hanging from the ceiling on a cord finished the view. We're here, I thought to myself.

Unpacking a few blankets, Diana attempted to find a clean spot for the boys. Goliath happily snuggled in, thrilled to be along for the ride. The next morning, I was called on my integrity and principals and had to make a ridiculously hard choice. LEAVE!

Sitting in the tip of Texas, penniless, with a flat tire and no idea in our heads about what was next, we could not do, what this couple asked us to do. Calling Lori, I shared what had happened and she agreed that it would be wrong to do what I was being asked. So giving notice to the couple that we would be parting ways, we packed for a third time and waited the seven days until we could go back to Oklahoma.

Meanwhile in the very midst of this mess, a man named Ken was at the door. He had been the previous manager and was visibly drunk.

"Come on in," I offered, and, to my surprise, he did.

I had real compassion for Ken. He was a typical big old Texan that stood 6'3" with a twang you couldn't forget. What a teddy bear he was, though. I told him what had happened to me and he shared that the night before he heard a voice say he was going to die if he didn't give up alcohol and turn his life around.

To my surprise, after sharing my story, Ken was changed and headed to tell his wife. Diana and I often talked about Ken, saying if the main purpose for our going all that way was for Ken, it was worth every test and trial. Last time we saw Ken he was waving away with a big ole glass of orange juice in his hand. Straight juice that is!

All packed, our hearts light, we drove back the fourteen hours to Oklahoma. Although arrangements had been made for Lori's son,

Greg, to pick us up, bad weather made it impossible. During those next two weeks, we hung out with Billy and Shirley, and their three adorable kids.

Our little families had a great Thanksgiving. Diana offered a ham, and Billy provided deer meat, fresh beets and macaroni and cheese. The weather finally lifted, and giving even more possessions away, we were escorted out of Oklahoma with one small trailer filled with our belongings.

Arriving in Salina, the snow was so beautiful; it looked surreal. Greg and his wife had offered to let us live with them and welcomed us into their home as if we were blood relatives. Since they had three wonderful sons, our boys were thrilled.

A few days later Lori called and asked if I would wash dishes. She needed the help at her restaurant and knew we needed some money. After having had successful businesses I did not joyfully anticipate washing dishes. In other words, my pride (which I thought I didn't have) and I met. Lori had also worked it out that Diana could do some hostessing. Biting my lip, I mumbled, "Sure, thank you."

Within two weeks after arriving we were not only gainfully employed, but had been introduced to a man named Ken, who was a realtor. Offering us a chance to rent-to-own, he even offered us free rent for the first month if I could do some minor work for him. The little house was tiny but cute. I could hardly believe that within two weeks, I was going to be in my own home, after leaving Texas without a penny.

Not having a phone, no one knew the day we were moving into our new little house. The morning Diana and I left Greg's house the snow was falling at a good pace. Arriving at our new home, we moved our belongings in and realized we had two sons who had a habit of wanting to eat, but we had no food and not one dime.

"Something will happen," Diana said. "Yeah, we are going to be hungry," is what I thought and yet in a few minutes to our surprise coming up the walk were Lori and a cook who worked for her.

Their arms were full of grocery bags. There must have been over a dozen packed bags of food and household products. During our eleven weeks in Kansas many other surprises occurred, including several strangers walking up to me, handing me money saying they just felt like they wanted to. This always happened when it was most needed.

The restaurant I worked in was one of the prettiest I'd ever seen. The decor had been brought in from Mexico and secondhand shops. Bright, big, paper mache flowers f rom M exico g arnished t he walls. Spray painted branches with colorful macaws were mounted around the room. Only five weeks after I arrived in Kansas, I had worked from dishwashing to overseeing the cooking. Nursing my wounded pride, I had learned a lot about myself.

Being with Lori was wonderful; and Diana and I were content in our new home. Working away, once again came the order to move. I came home from work and told Diana more shifting was going on. Little did I know that just that day, Dorothy, Diana's Mom had called.

"Diana, if you guys ever decide to come home, we'll help you in any way we can. We sure do miss those grandsons." she said.

As Diana was recounting the conversation to me, to my amazement, the owner of our house came by and said, "Would you be horribly disappointed if I sold the house? We wouldn't leave you in the cold. There's a mobile home I think you could move to." Even I can take a hint. "Call your mom back" I told Diana.

Briiiiiiiing! As the phone rang, we could hardly wait for her mother to answer. Memories of loved ones and precious times flooded my mind.

"Hello? Yes, Diana, I was serious!" said Dorothy.

"Well, Mom, we will take you up on that offer."

"Great, I'll tell Dad." Dorothy commented and with that Diana's mom hung up the phone.

Counting the stay at Greg's, this was our sixth move in four months. Thank God Diana was having a healthy pregnancy. I was amazed at the way she could hustle a tray filled with several dinner plates, up and down stairs to the banquet rooms. After all the moves, packing was not a big chore, and as always, the hardest part was saying goodbye.

18

Homeward Bound

We started out on our long trip back, but this time we had a moving company haul our few belongings. It was so nice just to pack clothes and jump in the car and go. We had grown to love Kansas but the thought of being close to family and grandparents was wonderful. It had been a terribly busy four months, but oh, what an education we'd gotten!

When we left Kansas, we knew our windshield wipers didn't work, and we were trying to outrun a storm. We would have had them fixed, but we had already sunk a bundle into getting the lights fixed and didn't have the extra money. After driving all day, we pulled into Dalhart, Texas in the middle of a snowstorm.

At the motel I discovered the radiator was cracked at the top, around the cap. The car was over heating, and I felt fortunate to have made it to town. Catching the news, I was not thrilled to learn, we were in the middle of severe weather with more snow on the way. The following day was spent in our motel room, as there was no way we were going anywhere.

That night, Diana, and I both awoke at 2 a.m. "Do you think we ought to head out before the storm gets worse?" Diana asked. "I don't know, but we could give it a try." I agreed.

To this day I really believe little Goliath helped save our lives. With the car packed and engine running, Diana called Goliath. He was nowhere to be found. We even drove up and down a two-mile stretch calling,

"Here boy, Goliath, come on!" But Goliath was not to be found. Since he had always come whenever we called, we were really surprised.

Finally, I said, "Let's go back to the room. We can't leave him here." I also saw that in about 10-degree weather the car had overheated. Unloading the boys and carrying them to the room, Diana and I were joined by Goliath the moment we were all back in the motel room!

Later when we found out the true condition of the car and how bad road conditions we were so glad we went back to the room.

The next morning, Diana said, "What are we going to do?"

"I can't do anything," I said angrily.

"Well, we could be getting the car fixed while we're snowed in, then it would be ready by the time the storm lifts." Diana retorted.

Wonderful! Just wonderful! It felt like nine degrees outside as I headed out looking for a radiator shop. I was sliding down the street looking for a gas station or somewhere to ask directions.

I couldn't see anything because of not having any windshield wipers. Hanging my left arm out the window I tried to wipe off the windshield over and over. Frozen, and blinded by the snow I had to pull over. Sliding into a parking lot, I found myself at a donut shop. The man was in the process of closing the shop due to the storm. I felt like I was in the Twilight Zone.

"Hey buddy," I yelled. "Do you know where there's a radiator shop?"

"You're in luck," he replied. "The only one who works on radiators is right across the street. It's a gas station, but they do that kind of work too."

Hoping the car would start, I turned the key and barely cranking over, I slid across the street, where the car died. Inside the service station a huge cowboy was sitting in his chair.

"Can I help y'all?" he drawled.

"Yes. It's my radiator." I said in frustration.

"Well, Tex should be in soon," and with that this good ole boy struck up a conversation about storms in the year 1902 or something.

My mind was obviously on a stranded family. Four hours later, after Tex arrived, the man offered me a ride back to my motel. He said Tex would call me as soon as he finished later that afternoon.

When I got back, pregnant Diana was frantic. Day two of constant commotion with two small boys, the storm, and the discovery that there were no taxis, no cars for rent, and no way to get food was driving her nuts. At six, I gave up hope that I'd hear from the gas station guys that day. Meanwhile Diana had discovered a market close by who would deliver groceries.

The night passed with no word from the Texans, so by nine the following morning, I called the police. It was the only way I could get a ride back to the gas station. Tex had fixed the radiator, but to let the sealant dry they had to leave it out overnight. So now, here I was again, waiting for Tex to show, to install the radiator. I wasn't allowed to install it because of insurance reasons. The snow was lifting a little and all I could think about was getting out of this town.

Crossing the street to the laundromat next to the Donut shop, I loudly offered money to anyone who would give me a ride to my motel. It's incredible how a room full of people can suddenly go deaf. Declaring it a shame how a man could fight a war for his country but couldn't get a ride five miles down the street I attempted to shame someone into helping. Raising my voice with each new comment, finally, the owner of the laundromat offered some assistance.

Diana said he was probably afraid I was about to come unglued if I wasn't already. Asking the man who gave me the ride to the hotel to hold on, I bundled my wife, kids, suitcases, and the dog into his car and requested that he now take us back to the gas station.

I figured if I parked the whole family there at the station, Tex might get off his duff and do something. It worked. Hurrah! "I guess Tex isn't coming in today," the other tall Texan offered 'So maybe I better do it so you folks can get goin." Getting the radiator back in place the good ole boy threw me the keys and pointed to the car that was out in the gas station parking lot.

I jumped behind the wheel and turned the key. Nothing! Dead! Dead as a doornail! NO LIFE! Are you getting my drift?

Numb, I said, "Come on Mom, grab the kids. We're going to this little cafe next door, feed the kids, and discuss this situation." Diana was totally silent.

A young man visiting his wife, who managed the cafe, overheard our conversation, and said, "Hey, I'm a mechanic here in town. I've got a shop to work on it, and can get it towed over there, no problem." Coincidence? He fixed the car in under two hours and only charged us twenty-five dollars including the tow. The car was fixed by eleven so with gaining an hour of time heading to New Mexico, we decided to leave right away. God bless that little couple. Heading out, we just knew our troubles were over.

Within ten miles we ran into traffic and the worst road conditions that I'd ever driven in, in my entire life. Diana was now over six months pregnant and how she endured all those bumps only God knows. The road was so narrow that two rigs could hardly have passed going opposite directions.

A snowplow had only managed to chop up all the snow, which had then frozen. Our Audi's frame was in constant contact with the ridges left by the snowplow. If you've ever gotten a flat tire you might get an idea of the conditions. To add to the overall view, we had no chains and still no wipers. The snow had stopped falling but the rigs going by marred the visibility, as they threw shovelfuls of dirty slush on the windshield. Our little Audi had a sunroof, so with no other choice, Diana 7 months pregnant stood on her car seat and hung out the top wiping her arms back and forth like wipers.

There was no way to turn around, and as we passed more than one car that had slid off the road, we crawled at a snail's pace. The temperature was around fourteen degrees; and I know Diana got slush directly in the face several times when she didn't duck back inside the car fast enough. We averaged ten miles an hour and it was brutal.

Seeing that the Tucumcari motels were sold out of, we made the decision to go as far as Santa Rosa. We were now on a bigger highway. Before we left Tucumcari, we found that our car frame was solid ice, and there were icicles above the tires. In thirty minutes, we knew there was only about an hour of daylight left. Seeing a sign indicating a gas station five miles away, Diana and I heard a clunk. It sounded like the whole transmission was gone. Somehow, the car was still running, but oh, it was hurting. It sounded so bad I thought the engine would blow at any minute.

That was the longest five miles I've ever driven. Pulling onto the off ramp, we saw one dinky, run down station filled with cars and trucks. Most of them were waiting out the storm, or so they thought. It was getting colder and colder. We had a flat tire and discovered that our tire jack was broken. I began frantically asking people to loan me a jack. Finally, a young man from my hometown of Fresno, CA. offered me his. The spare tire in place, we had about twenty miles to go and our lights were not working regularly.

Jumping behind the wheel I turned the key. Repeatedly I tried to get it to turn over and finally, the battery was almost gone. By now I was quiet, and Diana was tearing up.

Isaac said, "Dad, start it the way you did back in Kansas."

"What do you mean, son?" I asked.

"Back up and do it, Dad!" Isaac said again.

Suddenly, I knew what he was trying to tell me. When the battery was low, I would turn the key on, pop the clutch, and off we'd go. Looking at Diana, I said, "It's our last chance." Diana held her breath, Isaac cheered, and even Isaiah joined in as the engine barely started. Out of the mouth of babes!

We all sang songs and cheered as we beat it down the road for Santa Rosa. It took us an hour to go the last twenty miles. Pulling into the town, we saw literally hundreds of trucks everywhere.

A Holiday Inn was the first motel on our left, and I told Diana to run and go get us a room. Within a few minutes all their rooms were gone, and we had gotten one of the last ones. There were people sleeping in the hallways, on the steps, sprawled on couches in the lobby, you name it. The National Guard were called out, and Santa Rosa was declared a national disaster area.

Well, here we were, our fourth night on the road, and we were only as far as New Mexico. Our money had dwindled from six hundred dollars to less than eighty and we were in a motel paying forty a night.

"Mother, Help!" Diana cried out on the phone. Feeling like college kids calling home, Diana explained the situation.

Dorothy, Diana's mother, was so neat. "I'll send you our credit card numbers and don't you budge until those roads are safe. Don't take my grandsons on those roads until the storm has passed."

Later, Dorothy called and said, "I talked to Ivan and we figured you may need some cash. We'll send some of that Western Union too."

Now that Grandpa and Grandma had given us strict orders, along with financial support, we decided to take a forced vacation. Snow fell for the next two days straight. We could see the highway from our room; and we were told that traffic was backed up in several cities. Schools had been opened for people who were stranded to sleep at.

The snow that had been so deadly while on the road was breathtaking from the safety of our motel room. We enjoyed the rest, lots of room service, and visiting others who were stranded. Diana talked with a trucker who had taken the same highway that we had taken out of Dalhart Texas. "I've driven over forty years and I've never been on a road that bad!" he commented.

By the end of the sixth day after leaving Kansas, we were ready to be on the road again. Clear skies, Wow! Nothing can stop us now! After spending the night in Arizona, we started out at five in the morning for arrival day home. Laughing hysterically, Diana headed out the sunroof as the worst rainstorm to hit California began to poor in on our heads! We made it through the Tehachapi mountains into Bakersfield. Wipe, Wipe, Wipe. What a trooper!

19

Moving, Moving, Moving

Our welcome home was wonderful. My in-laws, Ivan, and Dorothy, welcomed our family into their home. Diana and I started looking for ways to meet our needs. Since we needed a place to live and a job, it seemed to make sense to apply for management jobs that might include housing. It was incredible, not one reply to our job applications.

Once again, we began house hunting. We found the cutest little white house on Myrtle Street, placed exactly halfway between both grandparents. Diana's parents, sticking to their offer, continued to help us with mental and financial support. Selling the Audi, Ivan offered us his Datsun. Set now with a home, the start of a business (Diana decided to take an ad out for handyman), once again we were on our way.

On May 24th, the arrival of Israel Jonathan Nickell brightened our world. With the birth of yet one more son, waiting for the phone to ring for jobs was not enough. Enjoying the time with our new treasure was great, but oh my God, the bruised egos, the fights, the frustrations, over not understanding, how to make our worlds work financially and relationally. I even took a job setting up a Doughboy Pool with my nephews, with absolutely no idea how it was going to work but I knew my nephew David, was smart, and could help me figure it out.

Bringing all work to a literal halt for four weeks, Diana and I searched for direction yet again. Taking public assistance was hard, and embarrassing. All I knew, is that any job I tried without Diana never lasted, and she was having a heck of a time dreaming up ways to make money and create an income.

Ivan and Dorothy were still supportive, but with all the moves, and help and failures, it was getting hard not to want to hide.

A few weeks passed when I informed Diana, I really felt I needed to head to the coast, get quiet and try to hear direction. Supporting me yet again, in my journey to find myself, she shared that what money we had was supposed to last a few more days, but that if I needed to go, go! Buying some sunflower seeds and getting a cheap room, I waited, and waited. Then on the second day, I was sitting on the beach, on a huge rock.

All I can say, is it seemed like the whole beach lit up, and I knew someone was listening to my heart. Taking a path towards the street. I thought I was heading back to my hotel room but instead, as I looked, I saw a help wanted sign in the window. The sign advertised for a maid and I thought to myself, the sign says maids, what does that have to do with me?

Feeling urged to head there anyway I did. Walking up to the front desk, I inquired if they needed a manager, as I had seen a sign hanging in the window.

"No, just a maid," a man said.

"Well, my wife and I are looking to manage something."

"Get his number," a lady's voice yelled from the back room. Getting home, I sheepishly informed Diana, that I had not found a job, but had left my name, with a couple at a motel looking for a maid!

Within a few days, the phone rang, and Diana and I could not believe our ears. Would we please come manage a motel, in Cayucos California, overlooking the beach! What a dream come true! A real job, we could do together, including an apartment, only three hours from where our relatives lived, and the boys would love it.

Once again, had anyone told us what was ahead, I'm not sure I would have moved to the coast. Oh, it was beautiful enough. Who wouldn't want to live one block from the beach in your own private house complete with amazing views, the smell of the ocean, and seagulls soaring overhead?

Moving in the air was amazing, the seagulls' cries were music to our ears, and building a little fence, so that the boys could play in their own yard, we seemed set for good.

Meanwhile Diana and I discovered that our idea of manager and the owner's idea of manager were two totally different things. For the first two months Diana and I worked every day, all day, and were on call at night. We did all the work for the motel. Although it was small and had 17 units, that's a lot of beds to change.

Originally, the couple had told us that they had maids, laundry people, and maintenance and that our job was to simply rent rooms, and maybe help in one of those other areas occasionally.

On occasion Diana or I would get to the beach for walks. Since it was the slow season, occasionally, we would get visitors from the valley. October through December, the months flew and at Christmas Dorothy and Ivan came over and brought Isaac and Isaiah two motorized motorcycles! Oh, how the boys loved those. With Christmas Eve approaching Diana and I were surprised to find no business at the motel. So, we prepared for a quiet holiday.

As I went to close the office and lobby Christmas Eve, I sensed something strange. I was bending over to unplug the Christmas lights when my eyes saw a pair of boots; and it startled me, as I had not noticed anyone upon entering the lobby. Sitting in the corner was a person who made Charlie Manson look like a choir boy.

Taking a deep breath, I listened as this man pointed at the Christmas ornaments while saying, "See those worlds? I've been to every one of them. I have been all over California, up and down the coast. I died along highway 101 at least seven times."

At this, I came to the house and said, "I think Satan is setting in our lobby. Come on Diana, let's go over there, you won't believe this." No kidding: this was one character who had lost his mind.

Diana and I went over to the lobby and spoke with him a little while longer. Gene was his name; and as he continued to blurt out violent statements, we decided to call the police. As I was calling, Diana did the only thing she knew to do. "Gene, do you want help? A sandwich? Something to eat. A new life?

"NO, NO, I don't want that."

I told him since we couldn't help him, he had to go. The police arrived shortly, and even though we pointed out which direction he'd gone, they could find no one. Diana saw Gene the next day in San Luis Obispo, by a traffic light, talking into the air and to anyone who would listen.

In January, the city of San Luis Obispo mailed out labor laws for motel owners. The motel owners had received a copy of the labor laws; and knew darn well it was illegal to work both of us twenty-four hours a day, for four months with no breaks for six hundred dollars a month. Giving us notice that they were broke and wanted to lay us off our security flew right out the door once more.

Here we were being tested yet again. With a thirty-day notice we owned little and had nowhere to go! For weeks we applied at every motel up and down the coast, we even checked hotels in the mountains above Fresno. Nobody had the right set-up for a family of five. Deciding to take only what fit in our car, we had a yard sale trying to downsize even more, and make money to move on.

On one of our trips looking for a new job we had trouble with our car. It took us eight hours to limp it from the coast to the valley which was normally a three-hour trip. Having to put it into the shop, my sister's husband offered to let us use his second car. Now as thankful as we were, I was determined that I wouldn't let anything happen to this borrowed car, as car trouble was Sam's worst pet peeve.

Driving back to the motel we discussed how we just had to trust and if it came to the day we were supposed to leave and we didn't have anywhere to go, so be it. Pulling up to the motel I parked the car. As we unloaded suitcases Isaac and Isaiah headed for their play yard and we stopped to take a deep breath. "Well, let's unload Israel and get back to work," I said.

With that done, we put the baby in his crib and called the boys in for a nap. We proceeded to head for the office door, turned and looked again past our little house to the beach. Suddenly, our borrowed car took off. It went across a driveway, down a planter, over a curb, and out of sight. The minute it started rolling I ran after it. Shouting to anyone below to watch out, we watched as the car teetered over a curb and on to a street below. Missing two people and five houses it smashed into an old MG that someone had meant to restore but never did. "WHEW!" Thank God no one was hurt.

Could anything else go wrong? Telling Diana to call our brother in-law, then the insurance company. Waiting for Sam's voice to come on the other end of the line, Diana hoped he would not be to upset. "Sam, you're not going to believe this." After hearing the whole story and that we had insurance, Sam was very understanding.

Now that our car was repaired, we used it to get around while Sam's was being worked on. Packing our car with every belonging, the day had arrived. There we were once again, nowhere to go, no job, willing to work, and anxious to see what would work out.

Oh, Lord! Since I gave You my life, my path has not been easy. Never dull, never boring, exciting, full of life, but not easy.

Arriving in Visalia, for the next couple of weeks, we bounced around and stayed with several people. Finally, depressed and wondering if we weren't completely out of our minds Diana and I, our three sons, and our few belongings pulled up to a local park.

Weeping, Diana confessed to me that all she knew was that she still loved me, and no matter where we ended up, this was not about blame. We had tried everything we knew how, and still were not stable.

Setting in Houk Park, in Visalia, with a car on empty, seven dollars to our name, no food, it was a reminder of where we had started our lives together, homeless, under a tree. Well, at the least the boys should see their Grandpa and Grandma, before we leave town, or figure out whatever. Calling Dorothy, Diana was thrilled when her mother invited us over to see the grandbabies, and then added an invitation to dinner.

After that we were invited to stay the night. As we had been in this position before with them, it was extremely hard for me when I believed through no fault of my own, we were in this position again. My pride was being stripped and it was horrible. For a few days I basically hid in a bedroom downstairs, not having a whole lot to say to anyone.

Every day, looking at a local newspaper for jobs, I was sick knowing that nothing usually worked for me up to now unless it was with Diana. Finally going stir crazy, I told Diana get in the car, and grab the kids to. As we drove away, she asked what we were doing.

"Looking for a house," I said. Not a dime, no job, and here we were cruising neighborhoods as Ivan and Dorothy tried to figure out how I was going to find a job, while hiding in a bedroom, let alone a house.

As we drove around there was one house that caught our eye. No sign was on it, but it was obviously vacant. Smack in the middle of town, it was a beautiful Spanish style home that was on the edge of what had been a very prestigious neighborhood years ago. With a park on one side complete with a memorial to Vietnam Veterans, and a gorgeous brick church across the street, it would be ideal.

Diana decided to call the county the next day, to see if she could find out who owned it, by its address and since it was Sunday, we headed back to Ivan and Dorothy's.

The next morning, after getting a name and phone number, Diana made the fateful call.

"Hi, my name is Diana Nickell, and I noticed your house is vacant. What plans do you have for it?" After hearing they had just been talking about how it shouldn't be left vacant, Diana explained the facts. "We have no money, no job, and no furniture. We are a family of five and we need a home. We will look for work immediately."

Diana, Dennis, and their three sons

At that, the woman on the other end said, "Meet me there at 2:00." Around 1:45, as we were getting ready to go, we'll never forget Diana's precious father who has basically operated in the realm of logic and fact.

"Where are you going, Honey?"

"To look for a house, Daddy!"

"With no money, Honey?"

With a concerned look Diana's father muttered something about good luck!

Arriving with our three sons (as spiffed up as I could get them) we were shown a beautiful home. Hard wood floors, 1930's glass blocks in the kitchen, even down to a special built-in tile fountain in the solarium back porch.

A separate Spanish garage was out back, with stairs leading to an Italian style roof with an amazing view the city.

"What do you think?" said the nice lady.

What could we think? I replied, "It's beautiful!"

"When would you like it?"

"Well, I explained to you about our situation," Diana reminded her.

"Oh, don't worry about the rent. When you get a job, you can pay me four hundred dollars a month. Would you like the keys now????"

"Would we like the keys now?" You bet!

As we continued to visit, Diana shared that her maiden name was Hershey and come to find out, the houses owner knew Diana's father; and Diana had even gone to school with her son.

I can't tell you the expression on my father-in-law's face when we arrived home and Diana tossed the keys on the table.

"What's that?" he said.

"The keys to our new home, Dad. Want to see it?"

With Diana's mom laughing and the children dancing, we immediately went back to our new love nest. After a thorough tour, Diana's father shook his head, and walked to the back of the property and back, still wondering how this could be.

I'm not saying it has been easy for either of our families to understand the way in which we live. It was not until many years later that we figured out that I had suffered post-traumatic stress from my time in combat in Vietnam and we really didn't understand why our world was different.

Be that as it may, here we were with an amazing home, a bright outlook, and hope was in the air.

Our three sons were growing, and I did any odd job I could get my hands on. During this time, the country was going through a great recession and our county had over twenty-five percent unemployment. One of every three families received aid whether it was welfare or food stamps. Going through three weeks of training to be a driver for disabled people I was told, I could not be hired as they were only going to hire all women to fill government quotas.

This was a very trying time and it was very hard not to be able to find a job and be independent. To be in a position where others help you constantly has got to be one of the hardest and humbling trials to go through. If you don't think so just try it some time.

During our first six months in our new home, we made enough to scrape together rent, but food was always a struggle. It seemed that no matter what right on time, some unforeseen help would arrive. I will never forget one time when one of Diana's uncles, came by and filled our cupboards with groceries that we immediately shared with another hurting family we knew.

Though we received help, we were determined not to beg. One morning we were totally out of milk and Diana was in the kitchen reading a Bible promise to Isaiah. There was a big horseshoe driveway that went right by the kitchen window, and as she was reading a friend came driving by and had his arm out the window holding a couple gallons of milk and drove off.

While on Hall Street, Diana and I met and befriended a woman named Judy. Her daughter was going through trials and she needed help watching her grandbaby. Well, after two weeks of watching this little boy I found out the neatest thing.

Years before, while in Terra Bella, Jackie (Mamma Lori's sister) called Diana. "Honey, please pray. There is a young woman on her way to the abortion clinic soon. We need to pray that this precious little baby will not be aborted." After Jackie hung up Diana did too, and do you know, that here she discovered, she was babysitting that same baby all this time later?

The school year was ending, and Lori, back in Kansas, had called and offered me work. I was willing to do anything to feed my family; and here was an opportunity. Unemployment was still extremely high in our town, so our choices seemed few. "Well, kids? How about Kansas again?" I asked. Excited for a change, all the family agreed this was what we should do.

20

'Round the Mountain

Deciding to take a train to Kansas, we thought it would be the thrill of a lifetime for our boys. My goodness, how could anyone be ever so wrong? Sorry, Amtrak, but this was our experience.

One day before we were supposed to leave for LA to catch the train, our transportation arrangements had to be changed. Ivan (Diana's father) stepped up and agreed to see our little family safely to the train station. The ride to Los Angeles was uneventful and there was an air of anticipation all around. Entering the big train terminal, we checked in our suitcases, (once again, everything we owned with us) and made sure our tickets were ready.

Ivan and Dorothy had agreed to send Goliath out via the airlines, as animals were not allowed on trains. Time marched on and before we knew it, we found ourselves boarding a 26-hour train to Wichita, Kansas. Bumping into everyone, trying to keep a hold of the stroller, two kids and a baby, and four pillows, we were off. Finding our seats, we settled in. We had requested "no smoking," so they put us in the last non-smoking row in an open train car that allowed smoking. Yuck!

Then we discovered because they hadn't charged us for the baby, Israel didn't have a seat. We hadn't bought sleeper berths, so we would be sleeping in our seats. When they advertised babies traveled free, we had no idea that meant, no seat. Oh, well, make the best of it, right?

Wrong!! Our car was the party car. 90% of the people were either drunk or quickly getting there. Smoke was so thick you thought it was a winter fog. As the day wore on, the booze flowed on, the stories got louder and raunchier. To make this a special test, our son Israel just had to be teething. Finally, midnight came, and the drunks were passing out.

Hooray! Sleep came. Then, in the middle of the night, transpired a scenario that only someone like Steve Martin could re-enact. Listening to all of this transpire about 2 rows behind us was unforgettable.

"Ahhh!" A lady screamed.

"What are you doing?" Someone else yelled,

"*!#*#!" The first lady screamed louder, "GET THAT %#*#! BACK IN YOUR PANTS!!! OH, MY GOD! He's peeing all over me!"

"Ahhh…He got me too." said a new voice.

"Someone call the conductor." Another person hollered.

Passengers were hysterical and conductors raced in.

"Here's a towel." Someone offered to the woman who was still crying.

"What did I do??" said the drunk as he was dragged out.

"You used the woman sitting next to you as a urinal," the conductor explained as they disappeared down the steps and out of sight.

Oh, my! Right, "See America," they said. Well, we did and that will do it for now thank you very much!

Someone wise once told me, if you don't get it right the first time, you just might get to go around the same mountain till you get the message. Arriving in Wichita, we were greeted by Kenny, a friend of Greg's. He was working at the motel as a cook the last time we were there and now was the full-time maintenance man. Since we had arrived around 11:00 at night and still had an hour's drive to Salina, we went straight to our motel room upon arrival.

Waking up to a beautiful spring day in Kansas, it felt great to be alive. Visiting Lori over coffee, the events of our train ride were told amidst laughter and giggles.

"Well, here's the plan kids. Dennis, you're going to paint this motel for me. On days that Ken has off I may use you to do maintenance." said Lori.

"Sounds great," I replied.

"Diana, I have an opening on Sundays at the front desk. Would you like to work it?"

"Yes, absolutely." She replied.

We knew that Lori would keep our hours different so one of us would always be available to be with our sons. Remembering the huge swing set and the big lawn the motel had, the older boys were out the door in a minute headed to play. Memories quickly returned of how kicked back and nice the Midwest was. Diana and I were prepared to stay.

Diana applied for a waitress job at the 24-hour truck stop across the street from the motel. Hired within two days, Diana explained she could only work after 4:00 in the afternoon, and not on Sundays. No problem they said. I was in heaven since I basically was in solitude. Every day I would get up and see what room Lori needed painted, and she would tell me over a cup of coffee, a few hugs, and a "Have a nice day, Honey!" After that, I would paint the day away listening to cassette teaching tapes. Oh, what a wonderful growing time.

When I was done painting, Diana was now running herself around the coffee shop tables from six p. m. to two a. m. in the morning, five days a week. You talk about a mission field: we had sweet people, hurting people, and crazy people. If you ever want to see a soap opera, just get around a bunch of waitresses. I think the owner's son was the only stable person there. When we got an opportunity, we tried to meet others and help where we could.

The boys were having the time of their lives. Since Diana worked until two in the morning, she'd get home and crawl in bed by three. That was always after a shower because it seemed everyone in Kansas smoked. She would come home just stinking. After a quick shower she'd fall into bed with me. Then at six a.m. I would leave to work. It was nice living right there on the motel premises, and while Lori graciously gave us free rent, we tried to save for a house.

My sons would pop up at about seven. Hopping on Diana and dragging her out of bed, she walked down to the motel coffee shop. There, Diana would purchase fresh home-made cinnamon rolls, go back to our motel room, crawl into bed and sleep till about ten a.m.

The kids watched TV while she slept. Then around ten they would all head outside to swing, take walks, visit me for a few minutes, or go to town to shop. Around four in the afternoon, Diana would start dinner. We'd all have a family dinner, and then off to work she would go.

Lori gave Diana her car to use so she wouldn't have to walk home when her shift ended in the middle of the night. Days flew by and there were many wonderful moments of visiting.

After about six weeks Diana and I rented the cutest house on a little cobble-stoned street where the trees met and made a canopy over the middle of the street. Getting our furnishings from an auction, we were ready to stay nestled in Kansas. The only problem now was we needed a car since we no longer were living at the motel.

On our first day in our new home, while I was at work, Diana looked for a car. She counted our cash on hand and it was five hundred dollars. Looking in the paper, Diana read, "Plymouth Scamp, maroon, rough but runs great. $500." Whoopee!!!! Within two hours we owned our own car. And it did run great. But, oh, was it ugly.

After Diana bought it, she drove up and showed me. Three of the fenders had holes where the snow had eaten through and the old, faded maroon color had a few places that had been spray painted to cover scratches and dings.

"What is that?" I asked.
"Our new car!" she said.
"You're joking!" I hopefully replied.
"I'm serious," she said.
"Does it run?" I questioned.
"I drove it here and it's paid in full."

"That's what counts," I said.

With that we decided to call it our California Raisin. Why, might you ask? Because it was wrinkled, purple, and ugly. But it ran great.

After finishing my painting, I had started landscaping the Salina Inn, and what a job it was. Lori gave me all kinds of wagon wheels, old farm tools, yokes, and tons of railroad ties. Add to that lots of flowers and the motel was looking up.

Around this time, I was beginning to crave stability. With the painting completed I wanted a career. Answering an ad in the newspaper I went and took tests to see it I could attend airline school. After several exams I was accepted! The only catch was that the school was in Washington.

Oh, my! What we wouldn't do to make sure we were doing all we could do to support our family. I had finished all the painting so giving a two-week notice, we called our relatives and told them we were headed for Washington in August and would stop by on our way through.

All the Grandparents were excited about seeing the grandchildren and responded in favor of our heading back West.

This time with a car we owned, money in our pockets, and a career ahead, we left Kansas at midnight after Diana worked her final shift at the restaurant. Hugging dear folk's goodbye, with our sons sound asleep in the car, we were headed for certain success.

After a week's stop in California, the Nickell family was headed for beautiful Washington. With dreams of flying all over the world for taxes only, we were determined to settle in as soon as possible. The airline school that had accepted me had all my financial grants arranged. They knew we were coming, and with $1000 we knew something would work out.

Our little Plymouth had driven uneventfully all the way out from Kansas and was now zooming up the biggest mountains in the US with no problems. Oh, we did see a little water from the radiator on the windshield at the very peaks. We also watched the temperature gauge climb to just below boiling and then right when it was needed the road would start descending and the gauge would plummet back to normal! Arriving in Portland Oregon, which was right across the river from Vancouver, we rented a motel.

Immediately, we bought newspapers and called rental agencies, etc. For three days we searched twelve hours a day. The story was always the same. It was "we don't accept dogs" (Goliath was still very much part of the family), or the rental agencies would allow two people per bedroom, so we needed to rent at least a three bedroom; and they did not have any available right now.

The same afternoon we arrived in town we called the airline school for suggestions. "Housing is extremely hard to find up here," they said. After all the searching, on the fourth day, we literally checked out the housing projects. The projects had a five-year waiting list. No one bothered to tell us about the housing situation before we got there.

Parking in a parking lot I looked at Isaac. "Son, what do you think? Mom has called every single ad in the paper, we have contacted every agency, and no door seems open?"

Little Isaac said, "Daddy, I want to go home!"

"Where's home son?" I wondered.

"Home is where Grandma and Grandpa are, my school, and my friends."

Sweet, sweet Isaac had so willingly gone back to Kansas and all, but in his heart of hearts was ready to settle down in Visalia.

"No," Diana screamed, "I just knew it." Having a royal fit, she wanted to move anywhere except Visalia. She was tired of people judging me, and our lives. We honestly believed that we had tried our best and no one we knew really understood.

After her fit, Diana apologized to the kids and started to get excited about Isaac being able to start back at his favorite school. Isaiah and Israel were ready for anything. I took a deep breath and said, "Ok, here we go."

Returning to Visalia by the fifth day we had less than an enthusiastic response. The consensus was we were at least a little strange. Of all the people to receive us wouldn't you know it would be my sister Penny? Without hesitation she seemed truly glad to see us and invited us to live with her for a few weeks. We only had about six hundred dollars left and I knew it wouldn't last long.

Getting up at six a.m. every morning I was out the door dressed in my best suit, not returning until late afternoon. After a week of no responses, this was the hardest time of my life not to go back to the crutch of alcohol. But, what a mighty victory! With a week to go and knowing we did not want to wear out our welcome with Penny, we started to house look, as well as job hunt.

One day we were driving around a cute neighborhood and again spotted an empty house. We called the county assessor and found out it was owned by a church. After calling the church and speaking with them, they agreed to let us rent the cottage until they found a new pastor. It had been vacant for some time. The price was only three hundred and fifty dollars a month (in 1988); and believe me, you couldn't rent a nice three bedroom for that. The very next morning, Diana, the kids and I were driving down Tulare Avenue when I said, "Let's pull in here."

The place was Good Shepherd, a state licensed facility for developmentally disabled. After I went inside, I came back out and had an absolute smile on my face. For the first time in weeks, I was happy. I was on the verge of putting an application in when I started to laugh. Seeing the precious people like we had the opportunity to serve before brought a big smile. Getting into the car I had to share.

"Diana, guess what we are going to do?"

"What?" she questioned, ready for anything.

"Why would I go to work for minimum wage at Good Shepherd when we could have our own care home again?"

Talk about blinders being lifted. Of course, that was the career. That was what we had been willing to give up so long ago.

As I shared my revelation Diana was so happy to see the joy in me as I spoke. Quickly, though, reality set in. More faith times. All we needed was a home big enough for eleven people, a state license, and about six thousand dollars. Piece of cake, right???

"Great," she said, encouragingly.

Within the week we were moved into the Burrell Street house. I was landscaping for my brother Jack, and still applying for other jobs all over town, and Diana was hired as a waitress at a local restaurant named Chippers.

The boys, knowing we were committed to stay in Visalia grew more happy and secure. What a wonderful house it was, and then, OH, NO! Within a few weeks we were given the word, time to move.

After months of waiting, the little church had found a new pastor. They felt so bad they offered us our money back to help us financially.

Diana and I house hunted for a new place to live with every spare minute. Isaac was in second grade, Isaiah started kindergarten, and Israel was three and quite a ball of energy. Once again Diana's father was involved.

Diana said, "Dad, we can't find anywhere to move!!! We have looked everywhere. There is one place we applied but they won't give us an answer until the day we are supposed to be out of the Burrell house."

Ivan responded, "Diana, you'll just have to go somewhere."

"I know Dad, but I believe the one on the line will say yes."

"Well, I'll help any way I can..." Ivan offered.

"Oh, good! Daddy? Two things! I need you to drive your car full of stuff, and Daddy?" (Now dads who are called Daddy by their thirty-three-year-old daughters know to be suspicious) "We need you to write the check, we'll give you almost all the money, but Dennis will get the rest from work in a couple of days. OK?"

"Sure, Honey" Ivan graciously responded.

Moving day arrived. Diana had to be at work at four in the afternoon and at one o'clock we were still circling the rental company waiting for an answer. We were out of the old place completely and still had nowhere to go.

Finally, around 1:30 p. m. the new rental company said okay and handed across the keys to an adorable condo. It had a back yard for Goliath, and we discovered the previous renters had even left a doghouse. This condo was small, homey, and provided for a very protective nurturing atmosphere. We had been through quite a walk and still had plenty to go.

Diana and I shared an open loft that overlooked the fireplace, and our three sons shared a huge bedroom downstairs. It was big enough for three twin beds. I had started full time home health care for a little grandpa who needed a home health care worker. For many months I helped this man while Diana waitressed. Once again there were great opportunities to meet people and we worked towards our dream of finding and reopening a care home.

During our stay at the condominium, we found the perfect home that we affectionately named the "Cambridge House." One day my brother Pat, who was now a realtor, gave us a list of about thirty homes, and as we started to leave, shouted out,

"Hey, I forgot one. Write this down."

Checking three houses on the list we were sorely disappointed; and Diana said, "Let's just look at the last one your brother mentioned."

Arriving at the address we were pleasantly surprised. The peach-colored house sported a cute picket fence and sat on a huge corner lot. We could see it was vacant; and there standing in the yard was a woman with her two boys, one who obviously had Down's Syndrome. Diana and I could not believe our eyes.

Stopping, we got out of our van and greeted the owners. After exchanging pleasantries, we walked through the home and found it to be perfect. The bedrooms were 13 by 16, a must for two people to have enough room. With three baths and an apartment size addition over the garage. Diana and I would have a bedroom fit for a king.

Asking if they would even consider a lease to buy option, Diana and I were thrilled when they said yes. The fact that they had a child with

Down's Syndrome they realized the importance of our desire to open a care home. It was destiny.

So many miracles took place it's almost hard to re-count them all. Within days of speaking to the owners of the house we had a signed lease agreement in our hands. But as the actual agreement day approached and our financial backer didn't feel they could allow us to use the funds.

They had hoped to hear a firm commitment from the agency that places folks in homes like ours, prior to releasing the finances. Heartbroken, we called the owners and told them that even though the funds were in our bank account we were not allowed to touch them yet. The owners of the house said sorry and put the house back on the market. The for-sale sign went back on the property, and Diana and I drove by again and again.

"I know that's our house!" Diana told me.

"Yeah, sure. Well, if it is for us it will not sell!" I replied.

"I know," Diana said.

Those were some of the hardest months we ever spent. Christmas time was approaching, and we wondered would we ever own our own home again.

Shortly after that, a day or two before Christmas, Diana ran into the owner of Cambridge House while grocery shopping.

"How are things going?" asked the owner.

"Well, we're still interested in your home if it isn't sold!" Diana replied, hopefully.

"Well, we did have a buyer, who offered full price and cash, but we just didn't want to sell it to him. So, why don't you give me a call when you get home?" Wilma invited.

One call later, one call to our backer, and one signed lease later, Diana and I had a move-in date of January 13, 1989. Once again, we were moving, this time hopefully to stay put for a long time. The big challenge now was supporting the home while we got it licensed.

Licensing takes a ninety-day process, and then the placement agency will hopefully start showing your home to perspective clients. At seven hundred a month strokes, we had our work cut out for us. Much of our money went to furniture, equipment, and start-up costs. Diana ran ads in the paper for me to do one-time cleanups and I also continued to provide home health care for the little grandpa.

One month towards the end of the ninety days we got the opportunity of a lifetime. Standing in line at a Starbucks, we overheard a woman talking about how expensive moving companies were and how she didn't want to pay so much to move to her new place at the coast.

After chatting we underbid the movers and were able to make a full month's rent in one day. It would save her a ton of money and somehow, we managed not to hear the words that she was moving to an upstairs apartment. In one day, Diana and I filled a medium sized moving van full of tons of stuff. Diana commented she never knew a small condo could hold fourteen dressers.

We loaded it, drove three hours away, unloaded it and by nine thirty that night, almost crawled into a Chinese restaurant we found open to eat. Slumped into the booth from exhaustion we agreed that it was the best food we'd ever eaten.

We'd made it the ninety days, we were all ready to get our license, and instead we received a letter from licensing asking, "Where are your three months running monies?" Oh, no, just a small matter of six thousand more dollars needed. In tears, Diana read the letter to me and I said, "Leave me alone!"

Walking back towards our garden I wondered how on earth we were supposed to come up with another six thousand dollars. Within a couple of moments, a woman's name came to me. Diana called her and within one day we were putting the full amount into a bank account per licensing's request.

Finally, with everything ready, we were well on our way to being reestablished. Four little seniors, all basically orphaned, a young mother with cerebral palsy, and her baby, who is healthy as can be, were the amazing folks who ended up at our wonderful Cambridge Home.

21

Happy Thoughts

Our dreams of staying in our wonderful Cambridge Home ended abruptly when after wonderful years of running our facility, home schooling, and being incredibly busy, one morning I went to sit up and my body physically would not respond.

Soon Diana and I were losing everything. Two of our clients left, which amounted to one third of our income. For months we struggled and did everything we could think of to keep our sinking ship afloat. Leasing out a Pizza Parlor on top of the care home, we tried everything we could to save our home.

At the same time, I was having serious chest pains and the stress just worsened. One morning I physically could not sit up and had not eaten in weeks. Visiting a doctor for a physical the first time since Vietnam, he diagnosed that stress had literally shut me down.

Not knowing what else to do, Diana called the regional center and in less than twenty-four hours, we closed our care home. We had been totally successful and blessed, giving all we could with our actions, love, finances, and did not understand why this all was happening.

Leasing out our home with a two-year lease-to-buy option and doing the same with the Pizza Parlor, we moved in with a friend and tried to find direction. The people who owed us money for leasing our home and the business did not follow through. They were deeply sorry but there was not much we could do.

So here we sat with a family of five with nowhere to go. I was still so sick with a relapse and was addicted to the stomach pills that enabled me to get a little something on my stomach. No income! Totally stripped (everything we owned fit into our van)! To add insult to injury, our precious Goliath died; and two days later, our other pet, Angel, got hit and died.

I will never forget when there was nowhere else to turn; we chose to turn to trust the one who made us. Isaac, Isaiah, and Israel, our three troopers, would all get in a circle around their Daddy, who they had never seen so weak, and snuggle me and pray for me.

One morning during all this Diana was absolutely compelled to start a business. Yes, you heard right, start a business, with no money, no supplies, and no experience in what she was about to do. Getting a briefcase (empty, except for a pencil and piece of paper), she called corporate businesses.

Explaining that she specialized in made to order custom client thank-yous, she designed to people's budgets, took half down with an order, and received the rest on delivery. That way she had the money to make the gift baskets, imprinted items, whatever they needed, and before we knew it checks were everywhere. I am not exaggerating when I say almost every single door Diana knocked on loved the idea and bought at least one gift basket.

Huddled together one night watching "Hook," Diana and I agreed we now had the name for our new business: Happy Thoughts. In the movie Peter Pan, Peter could not fly without his Happy Thoughts, and in Hook, those were his children. Since our sons are our treasures and have been the greatest gift in our lives, we decided to use that name to remind us of our treasures, who had helped inspire us when there wasn't much to smile about. Thinking of them always provides us with "Happy Thoughts."

Diana and I were not the only ones going through tests, so were our sons. They had been attending a private school, but when our finances went so did the private schooling. This was one of the most heart wrenching experiences of our lives. For years we had put every penny in the direction of their education, wanting the absolute best for them. Now making the best of the situation, we prepared our sons for a new school experience. Gathering in a little circle every morning we would visit and encourage our kids through all the changes.

Life went on, and with the boys in school and my strength slowly coming back, a new test was around the corner. We had thirty days to find a new place to live, and being close to Thanksgiving, we were just ready to see what would happen business wise that Christmas.

Once again, with no savings but believing somehow this would work out, we went house looking and found a beautiful little home with a swimming pool and fireplace for six hundred a month. The only catch was the landlord wanted first month's rent plus a deposit. So just like the good old days we put a deposit down hoping some how we would come up with the rest of the money.

Christmas was busy with little baskets, big baskets; and all the business was coming by word of mouth. Christmas was approaching, and now less than 3 weeks to save to get into this house. Charging Christmas presents seemed the only thing to do yet, we were feeling convicted that getting in debt was not wise.

Sitting in the living room one night, Diana burst into tears and called our three precious sons to our sides. "What should I do? We believe it is wrong to get indebted and yet if I don't charge these bikes there won't be any for Christmas."

"Mom," little Isaac, now ten, said, "That's simple. You can't do it. Don't charge."

"It's ok," Isaiah chimed in, don't do it, Mom." What love! What great kids. Christmas came and went. As always, due to generous grandparents, and relatives our boys were far from empty handed. Now the big test was on. Christmas had been good and Happy Thoughts was slowly growing.

Yet, we were still four hundred short, and the new landlord was adamant: no keys without the full amount. Packing our belongings, we prepared for the great moving day, still uncertain how all this was going to work.

The morning we were to move, Diana went outside at six a.m. to get the paper, and there on the porch was an envelope with a letter and yes, a check for exactly what we needed.

"Dennis!" Diana shrieked through the house, "Guess what? God did it, He did it!"

Much commotion was had as even the kids skipped around in circles. As tired as we were from all the battles, moving day was wonderful. Now instead of two bedrooms, we had a whole house again, with a fireplace and a pool, all on a big corner lot. Meanwhile I had gotten a landscaping job that was going to meet our needs. With thoughts of the business growing, we looked great on paper. Still the tests to come would reveal even more about ourselves.

Rain and more rain. It was a very wet January and instead of the twelve hundred a month income I had anticipated, I was fortunate to see anything. Meanwhile when I did work, the crew I was on was doing jobs as quickly as possible. Finally, the weather eased up and several good weeks of work waited ahead. But something was wrong. I was coming home at 3 o'clock in the afternoon and passing out. From time to time the old stress symptoms would return. Finally, we discovered that due to all the rains and many other factors, my body was saying "enough."

Just like most men, I was convinced if I could still crawl, I would provide for my family, no matter what. Repeatedly, Diana begged me to quit, stop, and cease! I was terrified that I must do all I could do to support my family. Awaking one morning with shoulders, arms, and wrists totally numb, I had to admit something wasn't right. The symptoms came after a day of putting almost five thousand feet of sprinkler system, in muddy ground in one day.

After about an hour, the symptoms lifted a little and I still reported for work, but thank God, the crew was rained out. By the next morning, my arms were worse, and we knew I needed to see a doctor. The prognosis: SURGERY! I had given myself carpal tunnel and injured my nerves. In a few weeks I had done the type of damage most people have only after years of overworking a certain spot. With both arms in braces and instructions not to use my hands, Diana couldn't help but ask me if I would rest now.

There was literally nothing I could do, and I finally realized I simply had to walk through it all. What ensued was a yearlong battle with workman's comp. After surgery, and rehab, and court hearings, two rehab counselors, two attorneys, etc., we emerged from this experience with hope and I was rehabbed into Happy Thoughts business.

There was lots of swimming and barbecues through the spring and summer months with lots of growth and many miracles for our business, Happy Thoughts. One day while driving along, the name of a business popped into my head.

"Diana, you have to make an appointment and go to this business now, today."

I was very bold and certain Diana had to do what I was saying, so even though I had no idea what to expect, she followed my instructions. The Result? A basket account for THREE HUNDRED baskets a month. The timing was crucial. The client's exact words?

"I can't believe your timing! We need your service."

Repeatedly through the growth of Happy Thoughts, it seemed we would make business connections in unorthodox ways.

Time was drawing near to move back home as the people who leased our Cambridge house decided not to buy it. This was a whole other story of faith and battles and on December the fifth, nineteen ninety-four our weary wiser family found ourselves circling our beloved Cambridge Home.

Entering the home with the weight of knowing the tenants had left us owing three months back rent we had no idea how we were going to pay for it. Within two weeks we discovered that because they had vandalized the house by pulling out towel bars and making lots of unauthorized changes our insurance was going to pay for all the past debt and repairs! It was incredible. If they hadn't been malicious the insurance wouldn't have covered the changes but since they had purposely torn some things up, we were totally covered!

Our Happy Thoughts gift basket business continued to prosper and grew in just three years to a successful company with over $50,000 sales in its third year. For several years, every baby born, in our main hospital was gifted an amazing welcome basket that bore our name, and life was getting good again.

22

Sinking Business

Why? Oh, why is it that when you just think you've got things figured out, you find out how much you don't know?

Christmas 1996 was a memory maker with lots of presents and the promise of an even better business year coming up. Diana and I had figured out that if we could have our biggest account pre-buy for a year, we could be debt free, have a great buying trip at the world-famous San Francisco Fancy Food Show (with Diana's parents Ivan and Dorothy), and build the business. Packing excitedly for the trip to the Mosconi Center, we imagined how many more corporate accounts we could sell and talked about how fun the trip was going to be.

Stopping in Old Sacramento on the way north, we breathed in the sites of the old paddle wheel steamboats and the old frontier town. Joy comes in the morning and I could hardly wait to confirm our next year's business with our largest account!

December, which was our normal time to approach this account to confirm for the next fiscal year, we shared our concerns that for several months we had become aware that they were not getting the baskets to everyone. Taking a survey at the local mall, and various places around town we discovered many of the minorities were not getting the baskets.

We knew at the time; and had even talked about it before hand, that if we made waves it might cost us dearly. As we checked the yearly birth count with what had been ordered there was a definite problem and breach of agreement. Thinking that the way through this sticky wicket was to be honest, confront, make sure everyone got a basket; we even offered a business deal where everybody saved money by bulk- buying for the whole next year.

Well, guess what folks? Here Diana and I were standing at the Fancy Food Show calling long distance as the purchasing person had promised an answer by that day.

"Order? Oh, No! As a matter of fact, we don't want your services anymore!"

To say joy was not her response just might be accurate! Trying to be the hero, she didn't tell me until after we were back in Visalia and we made an appointment with the purchaser. We had an agreement through the end of June, and we were going to expect them to finish the year! Well, they didn't, and what ensued were several horrible stress-filled months with the only nice memory of San Francisco being the great time spent with Ivan and Dorothy. They always had loved to travel and were fun on trips.

As March came around Happy Thoughts had another client who had demanded samples and designing meetings with Diana for two solid months, agreeing to make a major purchase. The account was to be five hundred items with a budget of sixty dollars each. This would be the largest single purchase we had ever accomplished.

Since two companies were involved in pulling this together, we were being run from one town to another; and we never would have imagined what was to come. After months of searching for special farm products, deluxe knifes, cowboy items, on and on, one VP finally set a day for ordering! Diana and I were so excited. Fifteen to thirty thousand-dollar accounts were not the norm for us, and this would be our ticket to making it through the other companies breach of their contract with us.

I will never forget Diana's face when ordering day came and we both expectantly waited for the call. Hearing Diana mumble something about getting back to them, she looked at me while wincing.

"They want to order one hundred cloth bags with their logo for a price of three dollars and forty-nine cents each." What a kick in the gut after months of meetings, design options, research and more.

What was wrong? Our products were tremendous, our service personal and professional; nothing had changed; yet we couldn't sell anything!

June was here and it seemed only a dream that last summer our family had been guests of Diana's parents for a wonderful paid vacation to Hawaii. Dorothy was retiring and to celebrate treated all the Hershey girls to a week in Hawaii with their families. Now, a year later summer was approaching, and frantically, we scrambled trying to figure out what was happening.

While I started looking for other jobs Diana filled out every form, she could get her hands on for a second mortgage for the house. Happy Thoughts was drying up, and the home equity was a way to buy some time, while we kept marketing.

Relief came as we managed to get a small second on the house and hoped that business would pick up. Diana and I marketed every other hospital in central California hoping to make up for the account we had lost.

23

Heart Attack!

Stumbling out of the bathroom early one morning, I was bent over in excruciating pain and said, "I need to go to the hospital. Don't call an ambulance I don't want to scare the boys." Diana helped me downstairs, and as she stuck her head in their rooms to say pray, I mumbled "be sure to tell the boys I love them."

In the emergency room our family doctor started ordering different tests to try to find out if this was indigestion or a heart attack. He gave me a huge cocktail of all kinds of upset stomach medicines and I watched as Diana took care of all the paperwork, and details. The pain was debilitating, and the morphine just did not seem to take away the severe pressure.

Later I discovered that the hospital had made several major errors. Tests that were taken to check different blood counts were not returned on time; and then the wrong tests were read. In the wee hours of the morning a nurse returned and said, "Whoops! I read the earlier test. You are definitely having an attack, but we have missed the special window of time in which a drug to counter what is happening should have been administered."

The heart doctor, who came by in the middle of the night, ordered more morphine and didn't know I had even had an attack and was having another and said, "Probably about noon tomorrow if this hasn't lifted, we might take a look, by the way how bad is it?"

"It's really, really bad!" I kept saying. From seven a.m. the one morning to the next morning was severe non-stop pain.

Morning arrived and Diana had walked out of the room just in time to overhear several of the heart doctors saying something to the effect that no one had notified them of the test results and I had literally laid in the hospital through several heart attacks without any intervention other than morphine.

Overhearing this, Diana later told me, she finally vented and told the two doctors that quite frankly she believed that my still being on earth was no thanks to them, and they better get with it.

Do you know those two grown men didn't say one word except for, "All right!" Within minutes my family physician, sweet Elizabeth, had shown up only to find out she hadn't been kept updated; and she asked to pray for me, as I was being wheeled towards surgery. How wonderful to have a caring friend and doctor who knows that there is the supernatural as well as the natural.

The doctors had stated that if the surgery took longer than one and a half hours there was a phone on the wall to use to find out what was going on. Permission had been given to do whatever needed done. About forty-five minutes after the original time, Diana was informed I had made it and great news.

The next four days were continued mishaps as I was lost in the shuffle and was supposed to be receiving intensive care level of attention. To those readers who are familiar with heart surgeries of any kind, if the doctors go in through the main artery in the leg, there is a twenty-four-hour period where they leave a plastic, hollow, straw-type of shunt in the leg right in a main artery.

After heart surgery, the patient, who is no longer on morphine but still on heavy painkillers, is supposed to have the leg weighed down and or tied so the leg cannot be kicked. If the patient were to kick the leg while high, they could bleed to death in about two minutes.

Diana later told me that while I was higher than a kite, she caught me kicking my leg at right angles, since my leg had not been weighed down, and I wasn't in ICU. When help arrived, the nurse on shift couldn't believe that no one had weighed my leg down. To this day I cannot tell you how that plastic straw didn't break that artery!

Thank God for Diana, as she literally stayed with me twenty-four seven, and cared for me during my six day stay in the hospital.

Day three, after the surgery, proved to be one of the most awesome days in our lives! Shunt removed, I was so looking forward to my first real walk. Oh, how we laughed and talked as I took my first steps holding the little IV holder. Ever so slowly I walked and we both were so grateful for the good reports and the time we were spending together. Finishing several laps around the nurses' station I was totally worn out and was ready for a good night's rest.

With finances gone, a prescription for no new major projects for an awfully long time, the words rest, and recuperation were doctors' orders. Great! Wonderful!

After faithfully working so hard we now were once again going through a wilderness experience equaled to none that we had ever been through.

Placing a call to Trish our best friend and right hand, Diana basically said put everyone on alert, no visitors for several weeks. Dropping by meals or helping financially was great but I needed complete rest and was under a mandate to not be disturbed.

Arriving home, the boys escorted me to a bedroom downstairs while Diana continued to make sure everything was taken care of that she could. Horrible thoughts of not being able to support my family yet again, drove me to put on a suit two days after I got home.

The boys said hi once or twice a day; and other than that, the house was noticeably quiet. As I read, and slept, Diana would report when someone would sweetly drop something by. There were just a couple of days left until the home was going to start foreclosure and a friend showed up at the door.

"Hi! Have you been praying?" he asked. "I was out in my fields on my tractor working and the Lord said you needed this." Laughing he said, I tried to argue with him, but he wouldn't leave me alone. This man handed us a check for not one, not two, but THREE months mortgage payments. Not a loan, A GIFT! It was the exact amount we were behind.

Meanwhile Diana continued to try to market anybody who might possibly need a gift basket; but it was abundantly clear "Happy Thoughts" was not happening.

Resting in the back room, I appreciated everyone's efforts, but I was so sick from the meds that they wanted me to take. Finally, a day before I had an appointment with my heart doctor, "Dr. Lively" I had a reckoning with my maker.

"I will not live the rest of my life sick! If you want to take me home great, but not sick!" You and I will just have to talk about it when I get there. So, with that said, I threw away all the pharmaceuticals that were making me so sick, I couldn't even function.

Telling my heart doctor I refused to live sick, he said ok. Then he ordered a stress test. Yet another reason to be grateful. The test showed I had the heart of a teenager, and there was no permanent damage.

In the natural though, even with these good reports there was a walking out period for my body to heal. Fighting extreme fatigue, muscle spasms that imitated the feelings of an impending attack, and severe indigestion, I had to continue to walk out my healing.

In October, we listed our home for sale and with our dear friend Trish, decided to head to Texas whether the house sold or not. I was ready to go, and we felt vomited out of California.

Life continued to happen, and it would take volumes to share, the insanity we went through in Texas. Oh, there were some highlights, and good times, but let's just sum it up with saying, that only one year, after moving to Texas, we were on our way back to our Cambridge home and family in California.

24

California, Here We Come!

Returning to California, we were lighter by one vehicle; Trish still had her Oldsmobile, and we had rented a Penske truck. Prior to leaving Texas, we had non-stop trouble with Trish's car, and it was acting like the transmission was going if you used overdrive. After many farewells to close friends and loved ones, we headed across country during a break in the snowstorms and took the shorter northern route.

It was perfect weather, and other than chasing all the cats "Christmas Kitty" had birthed, the only break down was by the Penske truck! The joke was we were all so worried about the car making it across country, and here the rental truck broke down.

Trish, Isaac, Isaiah, and Diana rode in the Oldsmobile while wrestling the four cats. Israel rode with me in the moving truck with… three puppies! Frito Boat, Pork Chop & Spunky were the three little puppies we had decided the boys could have, so our entourage of thirteen made quite a site. California here we come! Right back where we started from!

Driving up to our big beautiful 2500 square foot home, I couldn't believe all that had been learned and accomplished. We now were a recognized formal 501c3. We were convinced that a work was waiting in California, and that "there's no place like home."

Unpacking the Penske, we realized there were still a few details to tend to. The minute Lori's sister Jackie heard we were back she called and offered to set us up with anything we needed.

"Honey, now you come pick up some groceries and some hamburger meat. Do you need a stove? I think we have one out at the thrift store, you can just have it, Honey; and by the way, do you need anything else?"

Talk about being loved on! Then another call came in and Israel said, "Mom, remember Joel? His mom found out we needed a dish washer, and they have one we can have!" On and on everything we needed was provided for!

Walking through an old neighborhood one day Diana and I ran into an old neighbor. "Have you heard what has happened to Sarah?" Instantly my heart was tight as this precious Grandma filled us in. We had met Sarah when Happy Thoughts, the gift basket company, was first started. When we had moved into the little rental house on Vasser Street it came complete with a precious little neighbor girl named Sarah! She had beautiful blonde hair and a smile that wouldn't quit. This little princess would take Diana's' basket making scraps and leave little gifts on our doorstep. Little pieces of beads and ribbons were treasures to Sarah, and we quickly fell in love with each her. We couldn't out give Sarah; and her favorite hobby was to make special things for people.

As her grandmother shared what Sarah, now fifteen, had been through, grief is the only word that could express our sorrow. Trying to be brave for Grandma, Diana mentioned "Please, please tell Sarah, if you see, her that we love her and bring her by." Feeling rejected by everyone and everything, Sarah had been put into the foster care system. All I could see was the beautiful, innocent, little girl I had known; and heartbroken is the only word that can describe my sorrow.

A few months later, after Diana had been up all night, she had just laid down for a much-needed nap.

"Diana, get up, Sarah is here." I said.

Coming downstairs there stood our little neighbor Sarah! Now close to six feet tall, still beautifully blonde, and very much a woman far beyond her fifteen years.

Within minutes, she was sharing a heart wrenching story. Crying (something she hadn't done very much as it never did any good), Sarah poured out the sad story about where she had been and where she was going. As she talked about the rejection by her family, Diana's piercing looks were obvious.

With everything in her, she was conveying a message that should have been clear after twenty-two years of marriage. Asking Sarah to excuse us for a minute and stepping out to an adjoining laundry room I asked, "Are you thinking what I think you're thinking?"

"Well, what is everything we believe in worth if when confronted with a need, we do nothing?" Diana responded angrily.

"Hold on," I said and heading to speak with our sons, because I wanted to know their thoughts. The boys had a golden opportunity for selfishness for their last years as teenagers. Without hesitation all three sons declared that it might not be easy, but they gave their unanimous approval.

Arriving back in the room where Sarah and Diana were waiting, I asked, "Sarah? How would you like to live with us, for real? Have a real family, no more foster homes?"

Sarah's reaction was gratefulness mixed with surprise. She had been through a lot, but through her tears, she told me, "Know what? When I lived down the street from you, I always wished I could have you for my parents." Whew! Tears flowed, and then miracle of all miracles happened. To make a long story short, after a few calls, licensing hand delivered a packet to us to fill out; we were licensed in 24 hours, Sarah spent the weekend with us, and was moved in one week later. Anyone who knows the foster care system will know what a miracle this was.

Sarah's arrival day was only second to her entrance! At our urging, she playfully bounced into Isaac and Isaiah's room and jumped on the end of Isaac's bed to wake him! Crash. Isaac laid at a perfect slant as his bed was on the floor, one end of the bed crashed through to the ground. Not blinking an eye, Isaac smiled and said there are better ways to wake up and pretended to fall back asleep right where he was.

Welcome complete, the boys now had the fun of learning what the word sister meant! Isaiah came to the rescue; and since all the boys had gotten along with Sarah before, Isaiah and Sarah would sit for hours and talk. Israel had his own special place in Sarah's heart, and her in his, as he dutifully bugged her, but then would share walks to the mall to get crickets for Sarah's lizards and his frog.

During the week we got Sarah, "Happy Thoughts" opened its first transitional home. It was a place for hurting women to rest and be discipled, with one-on-one mentoring. This was not a home for a lot of people to be rushed through, but a refuge! So after almost two years, Trish was now moving, and our brand-new daughter Sarah had arrived.

For years Diana and I thought we were going to have a daughter. Israel was called "Sarah" in the womb for 9 months! Finally, after we decided we must have somehow missed what we thought was one of our hearts' desires, guess what gift arrived? Our Sarah! The delivery was a little later than expected but she certainly could not be any more loved!

As if Sarah's' arrival and the opening of another home wasn't exciting enough, a call came from a prime-time television program asking us to share about our lives. Can eagles fly? Butter melt? Birds sing? To understand why this was so special to us, you would have to know our hearts. We want to know God, to know His voice, and to be used effectively by Him for whatever He wants.

While all this was happening, our nonprofit Happy Thoughts continued to send out newsletters two times a year, help the hurting, we home schooled the kids, and counted our blessings!

25

Happy Thoughts Store

In Texas, Diana and I discovered the Greek and Hebrew meanings for the name Happy Thoughts: to go guide, lead the way, to create, invent, fabricate, to show the way! The meanings were exactly what our calling and lives have been.

As fall quickly passed, December 1999 was around the corner and everyone was busy, with lots of hot dog fund-raisers and preparations for the holidays. January was here, and before we knew it a solid year had passed since we came back to California. Peace had been made with the current mortgage company yet another time, and we continued to look for a storefront. The non-profit was dealing with so many clothes we needed a building.

In May, after looking for a whole year, we found two. These stores were special for several reasons. When we went out to find them, we didn't have $100 in the corporation.

The idea we had was to have two stores connected side by side! Of course, if one is looking for one store with no money, why not look for two? Finding the building, we asked a local ministry to help us with a thousand dollars to help us get in the door. Even though this had never been done, we were given the OK! The owner of the building then agreed to donate two free months for each store. I thought, how on earth we were supposed to put a used clothing store connected to a very fancy corporate gift basket store?

The design was from on high! Our family and close friends all labored away as we did the physical work to create an incredibly special place. The gently used clothing store advertised eighty-eight cent clothing, and yet, this store was presented like a high-end boutique. A 20-foot by twelve-foot-high mural depicted all the beautiful grape vineyards from the valley, as well as olive and orange orchards. Painted by Sarah, Ivan, Trish, and our friend Angela, we had farm laborers weep when they realized we were honoring their hard work.

In the center of the mural a simple farm worker lifted his hands to heaven while beholding the beauty of the hills and valleys before him. All the clothing racks in the store were hand made from wood from our friend's old ranch house. Isaac painted walls, and Israel and Isaiah built racks for hours on end. Spanish arches were cut in the walls between the two stores, and paintings of bricks and plants adorned the walls. The gift basket store was set up so that all profits, after taxes, were donated to the non-profit! We thought this would be a place to welcome the richest to the richest. It is said God has chosen those who are poor in the things of this world to be rich in faith. The days flew by and as things were needed, one by one, they were donated!

"Trish, we need carpet! Can you call and see if someone needs a tax write off? It's only nine hundred and fifty square feet for that one side." "Oh, now the carpets been found, we need a free installer and some donated glue!" Trish will tell you, after seeing how doors can shut, this was incredible. From donated paint to a $500 scale to weigh cheese and taffy, everything we needed was being donated. We were a businessman's worst nightmare on paper, yet it took less than $300 to open the clothing side and only about $3,000 worth of product bills for the gift side. The first rent was paid on time, all thirty-day bills paid within a week of being due, and when all was said and done close to $40,000 worth of services and items were donated to open the stores.

The year 2000 ended with close to $200,000 in tangible food, clothing, and services donated to those in need. Not to mention countless stories of specific changed lives of people who thinking they were coming in for clothes or gourmet candy, ended up healed and helped in more ways than one.

The atmosphere in these stores was so strong that total strangers would find themselves sharing their hearts, looking for answers to their problems, and we had the joy of directing them to The One with all the answers.

From the homeless to convicts, widows to the cities wealthiest, Happy Thoughts was used to bring joy to many. One precious lady named Laura, from Argentina, would spend hours combing through clothes, over and over, basking in the most wonderful instrumental music.

One day looking up from the register I saw to my delight another Spanish speaking woman who engaged Laura in conversation. Later the newcomer shared with me that she was able to help her.

Then there was the convict who was going to rob Trish. This young man had been let out of jail the day before and he had no money to buy his son a present, so he was casing the store.

Trish had greeted him with love and had an urge to gather up a stack of children's books! Approaching him, Trish told him that these were a gift from the one who knew him best.

Breaking down and weeping, this stranger confessed what he had come for and couldn't believe that someone was freely giving him what he needed; and he got so much more! Trish assured him how loved he was and locking up after the man left, Trish couldn't wait to share with us what had happened.

26

Time is Everything

Diana:

January looked so promising... Happy Thoughts had two full years' tax receipts and had proven itself a true help to the community with the lowest overhead of any charity around. As an organization we were prime for grants and our hope was that now with proven figures, Trish could submit for grants, and we could continue to grow.

Once again, our friend Arthur's words rang out "It's not where everything works out as we may desire."

Wham! The jolt from the full-sized truck ramming our Mazda was enough to literally knock the baseball cap off Dennis' head and into the dashboard. Burning pain shot through every muscle and ligament from the center of my back and spine. Crying out at the pain, I turned to see that Israel, who was riding in the back seat, seemed ok, as he had just put his seatbelt on a few minutes before. Insurance companies, doctors, therapists, drugs, tests, and more tests. The next six months were a blur.

Trish covered all the duties she already had, as well as mine, and there were simply not enough hours in the day. Happy Thoughts sent letters to anyone and everyone who had benefited from our years of service explaining about the accident. Not one reply. From local agencies to churches that had used our services for their clients, the only response was one get well card from the local chamber of commerce. **SILENCE!** It's amazing how loud silence can be.

Precious Trish didn't have time to write grants, and was realizing between the accident and the drugs, I was having serious memory problems! So much for marketing, grant writing, and any other type of activity to help us. Just keeping up with all the charity's demands, including training troubled youth, took 16 hours a day. Meanwhile our family was having their own challenges.

The boys had grown accustomed to their new sister; and let us just say Sarah' wounds and issues from her painful past provided opportunities for ALL of us to grow. Dennis had to deal with old Vietnam issues that never really left, a wife who couldn't be physically touched without great pain, a right-hand who was being driven nuts by my inability to remember what was said, and a sixteen-year-old daughter who was testing, testing, testing!

Farmers' Markets were going twice a week, our charity was running hotdog fundraisers at Wal-Mart and we were home schooling. If this wasn't enough on everybody, we had the opportunity to have a major fundraiser at the annual fair. I cannot honestly tell you how Happy Thoughts did all these things.

In late May direction from my oldest sister, Chris, was used to turn the tide on the physical battle from the accidents. She urged Dennis and me to get to UCLA to see a friend of hers, who she felt was the best in the business and would be able to help. As the good doctor said, "Throw out all these meds, learn the difference between good and bad pain, and change now, or you will be an invalid the rest of your life." This confirmed what I thought I was hearing in my heart as I had digressed to a state where I was taking heavier and heavier pain meds, to no avail, and even picking up a piece of paper shot pain through my back and shoulders. Leaving the Doctors office, I had decided no matter what, things had to change.

Driving home that morning towards our hometown I told Dennis what I thought I should do. Detox off ALL MEDS in the next three days! A call from Trish interrupted the conversation. "Guess what guys? We just got a three-hundred-dollar gift!" The gift was from a precious man who we trusted more than anyone on earth. It would take volumes to list every special detail of how, right when we were out of gas, needed food, or had another need, that mysteriously everything worked out.

Arriving home, I headed upstairs to my bedroom, the room where for over five months I had barely been able to dress myself and had not been able to simply make a bed. Now here I was with a vision of detoxing all meds in three days and scrubbing my filthy bathroom.

"You're kidding right?" I thought, as I stared at months of film and soap buildup, even though I knew in my knower this was no joke. Plugging in a Dottie Rambo tape, I will never forget standing in the shower scrubbing and screaming, "It's So Hard to Sing the Blues, When You're Doing So Well!"

Tears poured, as every muscle and fiber felt like I was insane and yet somehow it felt better to be doing something to help myself rather than be helpless. Three days later, after coming off all meds, cleaning my upstairs bedroom and bath I awoke feeling so much better. For the first time in close to six months I had my mind back and knew somehow things were turning around!

27

Transitions

Happy Thoughts as a charity was a resounding social success. We had proven that a faith-based charity could successfully network with government agencies as well as churches and other private charities puling from all the community's resources to help individuals in literally any area they needed. Financially we ended the year without outstanding debt as a charity and had kept our overhead at less than twelve percent.

Personally, though, Dennis and I had continued to dig an even deeper hole. There was not enough money to pay even minimum wage salaries, so we did not have money to pay our mortgage payments! The stores were just not generating enough as "fundraisers" to take care of even 1 minimum wage salary. It seemed every time we caught up, just got a new business lead, or a new promise of support these would disappear into thin air.

In December, a precious friend gave us part of her inheritance. She believed so strongly that what we were trying to build for our community was legitimate and needed. This was so hard to receive. After the friend's gift and some money owed us from the IRS, we were able once again to "start over" with the current mortgage company. Whether this was divine intervention and provision due to obedience, or mercy and grace to cover ignorance we weren't sure but knew that in time all will be revealed.

Bible studies started in our home where questioning, energetic spiritually hungry people would all gather. Once again, the Nickell boys and their sister Sarah would fill the house on Friday nights with friends, potlucks, studies, and wonderful times of fellowship. The book "Product of Love" was continuing to touch many, and Isaiah had typed the whole story onto the "Happy Thoughts" internet site to be enjoyed freely by anyone.

Christmas passed and with spring fast approaching many transitions were going on. Trish was now writing grants left and right while continuing to bring her personal caring touch to people one by one.

I wonder if any of the troubled teens, pregnant moms or even our corporate clients had any idea, or ever remotely suspected the price of the "gift" of Trish's love and service for them. Since none of us took regular salaries, we usually dressed from the "used" clothing store and poured ourselves out to the community without reservation.

By summer 2002 Happy Thoughts was horribly behind in rent. I had just spent another year physically battling all kinds of health problems and with so little help, the store was now open only five days a week. Not one of the grants submitted were awarded, and the store's owner had done all that he could. God bless Sam. This man had personally paid the price and taken heat from his business partners to help us, but finally was pushed to a place of having to see some money or close the doors. As the date grew closer for do or die, it was almost a relief. We had given everything we could.

D-day. Judgment day. Day of reckoning.

At 4:45, fifteen minutes before closing time, the phone rang.

"Diana, Diana! It's someone on the phone about a grant!" I yelled. The voice on the other end of the phone boomed out,

"How ya doin?" said the owner of a huge delivery company

After ten minutes of conversation, tearfully hanging up the phone, Diana gave me a thumbs up and called Sam the building owner.

"Sam, guess what?! A businessman who has a charitable foundation will be sending a substantial check overnight. Will payment for $5,000 be okay?"

Laughing, Sam seemed more relieved than me. So, with the ability to pay all suppliers up, (and a good chunk on back rents) Diana and I headed out the door. Locking the door to head home, like George Baily in It's a Wonderful Life, I said…

"Okay you old savings and loan, we're not through yet!"

28

VA

"Diana," my sister Pauline began, "Paul has a friend who has discovered that there is help for veterans like Dennis. Have you guys ever checked into the VA?"

VA: the sacred subject! Pauline shared that she and her husband Paul, knew of veterans who qualified for all kinds of help and that if deserving veterans did not apply the govt would use the money elsewhere. Calling the local VA a man shared that applying included lots of forms, being seen by a psychiatrist and with Dennis not trusting anyone, I knew this was not going to be easy.

Around this same time within a three-week period that Dennis and I were selling our "Happy Thoughts" gourmet products at the farmers market, veteran after veteran would end up at our booth, telling us their stories and sharing how they finally had some relief after receiving help from the VA.

Dennis had started wearing a ball-cap with the words "Vietnam Veteran" on it, with some patches representing units he had been with in Vietnam. Many times, this same hat had been used to draw hurting men, still injured from the war and Dennis would share his story of what and who had helped him. Even a congressman I had spoken with once had asked why with Dennis' service record and physical problems, he hadn't been to the VA.

One afternoon, in Happy Thoughts, I shared with Dennis, something I had learned from several of life's experiences, and most recently from numerous auto accidents.

"Honey, remember when I told you the most painful emotional day was when I faced the fact that, I had really been hurt from the auto accidents and I had to deal with all of that?" I began.

One day, I realized that due to someone else's actions I had been victimized and hurt. Helpless was how I felt, and anger welled up as I admitted to myself, I had seriously been hurt physically and emotionally.

Dennis listened and reluctantly allowed the first serious conversation about Vietnam and his wounds and we had been married twenty-four years. Agreeing to one VA office visit, and no more, my husband started down a path that ultimately would lead to much needed healing.

Busy, busy with Happy Thoughts, the fall season was yet another season of education of what people think they need and what they really need. The stores were not pulling their own weight and still we were busy helping many. We discovered that many people shopping at our clothing store wanted something for nothing.

I remember the time a lady in a Mercedes was so proud of herself for refusing to pay the full price for what she bought. Many of our customers would bag the savings and head to a restaurant nearby where we rarely could afford to eat.

Sometimes, the people we intended to serve did benefit. The older Spanish woman in the wheelchair was happily having the children she was with run 88-cent clothing to the register. Carefully picking out the clothes, she was having the greatest time and yet I could see she was in an old push wheelchair and dressed in used clothing herself. Moved by the scene, I asked the children with her, who all the clothes were for? Come to find out, she was widowed and lived in a farm labor camp. As children of neighbors would visit her, and offer to help with housework, etc., she would always send them home with a new piece of clothing. Mysteriously, the register rang some clothes at fifty cents, and many were never rung up.

The wealthy woman who drove the Mercedes was so proud she had saved a dollar at our expense and undoubtedly is one of the poorest creatures on earth. The Spanish grandma in the wheelchair will be rich all the days of her life.

My mother has a favorite Dolly Parton song: "The Coat of Many Colors." The lyrics are so true.

> "One is only poor only if they choose to be
> Now I know we have no money, but I was rich as I could be
> In my coat of many colors Mama made for me."

True riches are carried in the heart.

29

Freedom's Cost

The building our Happy Thoughts stores are in is going to be sold and torn down, according to the newspaper report. **What!?**

So Happy Thoughts stores were ending! Was this an answer to prayer? Dennis and I did not want to "give up the ship" so to speak, even though often the income was simply not enough. Closing doors was no longer the threat of humiliation, but perhaps a message of "job well done!" and on to a new assignment.

Meanwhile the VA visit had proved to start the long overdue healing process for my wonderful husband. Post-traumatic stress, Agent Orange. Diabetes, heart disease, hypothyroidism, High blood pressure. These were the words that identified the battlefields for Dennis now.

Dennis had faced his worse fears, including pride. To face the truth, he was only human, and had been horribly violated. No amount of pride, drugs, denial, or violence could change the fact that an idealistic nineteen-year-old had joined the Army to avenge the death of a friend. No longer his own man, he had become the "property" of the US government and was subject to their bidding.

When he was released from Vietnam, Dennis had a diagnosis of anxiety neurosis, psychosis, and verbally told he was a paranoid schizophrenic, with a destination of a mental hospital. The price that was paid by Dennis for service to his country was as real as the veterans who had come back physically crippled and maimed.

As Dennis acknowledged the cost an even deeper root came to light. He had not only come back totally incapable of leading a "normal" life, but he had also added guilt to the equation. Dennis blamed himself. Helplessness was the most frustrating feeling, as he didn't understand why he couldn't get rid of all the problems.

Some men had died in Vietnam while others came home with the visible proof of their sacrifices with missing limbs and all sorts of other issues.

The VA in Fresno has these words etched above the entrance,

> "Here is a place where the price of freedom can be seen."

How true that was. You couldn't see Dennis wounds. Finishing his service in 1971, no one even defined post-traumatic stress until many years later. Even the public had turned against these young men who had been so brave. Finally, after thirty-one years in the writing down of what he had been through in Nam for the VA, Dennis perception changed and so did mine.

How healing an understanding word can be.

"Dennis, anyone who was young and went through what you did would have serious issues, this was not your fault," the psychiatrist said. Then two psychiatrists confirmed and showed in real every-day words what Dennis still struggled with, how every day is an incredible challenge and now we really understood what a miracle his life is. The fact that Dennis has been given the grace to deal with such extreme challenges without being addicted to drugs and alcohol now, seemed to mystify the doctors.

"Well, what do you do? How are you doing this without drugs, and so on?" were their questions.

"I've learned that no matter how badly my mind freaks out, or how bad a fear attack is, it will pass," Dennis replied. What he didn't share was that what he had focused on, as his example of what should be "healthy, or normal" was based in his spiritual walk. Even though the mark was often missed he prayed and asked God for His Grace for these situations that seemed so overwhelming.

You see, we never talked about the daily battles for him and our family. We chose to look at all the good things and not the bad. From the beginning of our marriage, it quickly became evident that even though certain areas had profoundly changed Dennis still was incredibly challenged.

Yes, Dennis went from screaming six, eight, maybe more times a night to just a few. But the panic attacks and startle responses have never gone away. Yes, we had all the joys and true underlying peace that comes from knowing God and yet all of this was accomplished with much effort. Faith is a struggle, a fight!

The VA tests provided info to Dennis and me about how his natural mind literally still freezes when he is faced with situations his mind perceives as authoritative, new, threatening or hostile.

For many veterans, the invasion of a simple unexpected phone ringing is a reason to feel violated. Someone voicing a different opinion is the same as calling you stupid and all authority figures are there to harm you. We now understood why so few veterans stayed married and why the suicide rate is so high!

The VA psychiatrist asked Dennis to remember three simple words over a few moments. I was there for that test and I remember the words were pencil, orange, and bus. After telling Dennis the words, the doctor simply chatted about other things for less than a few minutes and when he asked do you remember the words? The blank stare on my husband's face said it all.

Mortified, and seeing such an obvious glitch, so clearly defined, we finally understood why he had never been able to hold down a job where we didn't work together. Between people thinking he was stupid from the way his memory worked, which was then compounded by the brain freezing in situations he felt threatened in, we had some understanding of why our family had gone through many of the trials we did.

As the psychologist researched, he found that panic attacks, interrupted sleep, and perceptions of everyday events that were colored by Dennis' time in combat affected every area of life. Social Security records showed an inability to hold down a simple normal job. The records also showed despite all these challenges he kept trying.

The VA then confirmed the connection between Vietnam and Dennis' heart attack. Shame and guilt and the burdens Dennis never should have carried started being realized and dealt with. The cost of freedom! His service to his country had come at a dear price and so few understood and even fewer ever said thanks. Veterans were spat on, heckled, and misjudged adding insult to injury.

The 4th of July 1998 in Texas a precious South Vietnamese man named Linh Vo met Dennis and gave him an autographed copy of his book "Dear Daddy." And we now had another view of Vietnam.

"Papa San! Papa San, you GIs are my Papa Sans. Thank God for You. I was on the first airlift out of Saigon as the country was being overrun by communists," Linh explained. "They overtook my family's village, and I had a split-second decision as a university student in the city whether to jump on a helicopter to freedom or stay. I was in the first arrivals to Camp Pendleton." Linh's father was a Vietnamese soldier who tried to fight the Viet Cong, and as a young boy, they had shoved a gun into Linh's head threatening him.

As Linh gushed appreciation for Dennis he freely gave him a book of his poetry to honor his service. "This book "Dear Daddy" is dedicated to all you Gi's my Papa Sans! I AM THE CHILD YOU WERE FIGHTING FOR," he wrote. The gratitude poured from this precious gifted poet was sincere. He was one of the oppressed that had been rescued and the gratitude was unmistakable.

Raising a family, Linh had built a life in the United States and experienced freedom firsthand. As a nation we worry about becoming involved in other nations problems but as brothers in the family of man isn't it heroic to want to help the oppressed? All we know is many Veterans need to hear Linh's perspective on America and Vietnam. So much gratitude for freedom! It was at this point that Dennis started the journey to accepting that serving his country, came with a cost even for those who made it home.

30

Wellness

Why, oh why, were we naive enough to think that as we headed into the second half of our lives, that somehow, we had arrived or at least earned the right to take a break from the types of afflictions and tests that seemed so "bountiful" when Dennis and I were younger?

With "Happy Thoughts" closed and our eyes set on a time of reflection and rest, we had no idea the fiery trial that was ahead. Like the fires in the national park, fresh fires often remove useless old dead wood. And like the droughts that proceeded the hottest fires, we were parched dry land, a tinder box waiting to be ignited. Originally firefighters tried to stop forest fires until a discovery was made: fires were good in the long run for the forest. Many seeds and nutrients were buried in the earth at the feet of the giant trees and only the combination of the ash from the fires and the clearing out of the "old" allowed the "new growth" to begin.

William, a friend from Texas with a very distinct accent, called and offered a gift that was straight from the heart!

"Dinnis? I know this man in Port Arthur who can heel ya! If yu and Dina can git out here... I'll payee for yuuu to see hum."

Precious William went on to explain that when he was a young man, doctors had told him he was extremely ill and was going to need to have his colon removed. There was nothing he could do about it! Well after visiting this man, who believed in healing naturally as well as divine, William was completely healed.

Learning that so many battles people fight physically are self-induced, whether on purpose or through ignorance, this brother had made it his business to help others find out they didn't have to stay sick! William had read a book, years before, named "Sugar Blues," that exposed how refined white sugar was so deadly for our bodies. William offered to fly us to Texas to see his special doctor hoping he could help Dennis get well.

Knowing that the years of fighting health problems had worn on both of us, the offer sounded good. It took Dennis a year to decide he was willing to see this doctor. Flying to Houston, Texas, Dennis and I drove several hours to the small city of Port Arthur. Looking for the address Dennis groaned when he saw the humble clinic that was located behind an old gas station.

Great! Flying halfway across the United States, we walked into a building that was more reminiscent of a bad veterinary clinic than a marvel of modern science. Trying to be positive, I snapped at Dennis to stop going by what he saw. Meanwhile I hoped William knew what he was doing.

Walking into the little reception area, I could see it was simple and clean. A few Christmas cards decorated the plain walls. A woman handed us some forms to fill out even though we had already previously sent in the longest questionnaires I had ever seen in my life.

Informing us the "process" included blood tests, that wouldn't be done for at least a day, we were invited to take a seat. The older light fixtures gave a soft glow to the wood-paneled walls, and I felt at peace about where we were. Then the most amazing thing happened that we had ever experienced from a doctor before or since.

A gentleman who we had heard was in his mid-seventies strode into the room. His natural, jet-black hair and the incredible shape he was in made him appear in his mid-forties. Vibrant positive and laughing, he loosened us both up. He then announced due to our coming so far and his wanting to truly help Dennis and me reach optimal health; he closed the clinic doors to walk-ins. He declared he had purposely not scheduled anyone else that day so that we had his undivided attention.

As this man shared his own stories and educated us on how eager our bodies are to be well, he gave us tons of literature with the latest holistic approaches to healing. Trained as a doctor of osteopathy, he was approaching illness from a kinetic understanding that believed all our bodily systems are so interactive you must treat the whole person.

Explaining that America was about the only nation that had the idea you didn't need to clean your own body from time to time this doctor ran tests that we had never heard of. Having taken great care to review our medical histories he proceeded to explain what he was going to do and why he believed it was the best course of action.

Never had either of us had anyone so thorough or gifted help us with our health. This man believed in healing. William had informed us that one time he asked this good doctor if there was anyone he couldn't help. The doctor's reply, "If they had breath, he believed they could be healed." With the dozens of friends William had taken to this man, he said the only ones who didn't keep their healing were those who decided not to do what the doctor said.

The doctor taught us about our need to "detoxify" our bodies from years of all the environmental stressors, and poor nutrition. In Dennis' case, exposure to Agent Orange in Vietnam, was also identified as a factor. We heard things that made sense physically and spiritually.

This man spoke wellness from the moment we arrived, and his only question was how best to achieve it. This was a far cry from so many "modern" doctors who simply treat symptoms and write prescriptions for chemicals that mask those symptoms. Dennis and I left that night wiser and determined to be well and whole. It might not have been instant, but it still was good news.

There was one small catch. Now there would be the doing, not just the hearing and self-discipline was neither one of our strong points.

After three days, Dennis and I flew home with our largest suitcase filled with various nutrients to detoxify, heal, and rebuild his body.

The regime included taking liquid drops on an empty stomach before you even got out of bed, to measuring and taking nutrients before, during and after meals throughout the day. Some nutrition needed to be taken alone and some with water. Some was to be taken with milk and some was to be stirred into an expensive clay type of mud that needed to be mixed and spread onto the bottoms of our feet and left on for 15 minutes before being removed.

What a bunch of work! Now we knew for sure why many people would much rather take a pill and cover the problem. This seemed like really hard work. I was starting to get suspicious there was a plan in taking us through all these gymnastics. We had been warned that when he started detoxifying, often the body would feel sick as toxins were leaving the body and our dear friend William must have said a dozen times to make sure to finish what was started and not to give up.

This reminds me how sometimes we think it's better to let issues be buried than to deal with them because bringing them up can hurt. There is always a cost associated with growth. Timing is everything and miraculously as Dennis did what the good doctor said, he felt better.

Knowing we couldn't be flying back and forth to Texas for follow-ups, I contacted the company who made the bioactive nutritional products we were using and asked if they knew anyone in California who used the same products. Only two doctors at the time and one was on a year sabbatical.

Dr. Jorge Moreno was the ONLY physician in California who was using these bioactive products that would get to where they were needed rather than be peed out. Leaving a message with a secretary I requested that if it was at all possible, I needed this doctor to call me. I had no idea how I would pay him. All I knew was that Dennis needed to finish the process he started. To my surprise, later that evening, I received a call from "Jorge."

Visiting for close to an hour, he agreed to see Dennis and that we could barter down the road. I hardly could believe it. He was kind, warm and personable, asking lots of questions and didn't seem in a hurry. Riding our Harley to Santa Monica to meet Jorge, Dennis was still a bit put off that he had to be part of his own healing. Many a lesser man would have given up and I continued to be the cheering section, pep squad and instigator. We continued to take this battle for Dennis health personally and seriously.

Pulling up to a beautiful office in Santa Monica I was looking forward to meeting this man. Dennis still struggled with the whole issue of being the center of attention. We both were from the old school of "take two aspirin and keep going".

To need someone's help is not a comfortable place to be. Well, here we were, Dennis and I like the odd couple, me so excited to meet Jorge and Dennis wishing he were at home in front of a good ballgame.

Dr. Moreno strode into the office with a huge grin and eyes twinkling. Attractive and athletic he exuded health. Heading straight for Dennis with right-hand extended, this man had a confidence and friendly air about him that made even my husband relax. Visiting away we couldn't help but notice I felt like we were all old friends. Laughter and stories filled the air. This physician had made sure to set aside three hours for our first visit and once again we realized we were in the presence of someone who was obviously in their God given calling.

"George" as Dennis affectionately dubbed Jorge, was a D.O. who was passionate about treating his patients from a wholistic perspective. Kindness and gentleness permeated this man and before leaving, Dennis was compelled to share with Jorge, that never had he ever met someone with more peace, and he was genuinely happy to have met him.

Preparing to leave, Dennis and I noticed a beautiful picture hanging on the wall. Staring at us was Jorge with his beautiful wife Yoli and their children. One couldn't help but notice, they all were the picture of happiness and vibrant health.

What a concept! If you are going to engage in a battle for your health, try finding someone who practices what they preach and is healthy.

31

Let the Games Begin

With a set monthly income and the Happy Thoughts stores closed, Dennis and I had been given the time that we thought would enable us to pursue our hearts desires without feeling stretched and pulled in so many directions. We were clueless that our own "home" was in such need of attention and I am not just talking about our physical house.

There is only so much time in a day and in our zeal to help others we had not taken time for many of our own basic needs as husband and wife. We had finally started to feel some relief with the small but steady income from the VA pension, but we continued to battle with the VA process and fought through numerous appeals.

During the first few months Happy Thoughts was closed we tried to work on some home projects. It seemed that with ongoing physical battles and exhaustion we both really needed some space. I have heard "steel sharpens steel," yet this was horrible. The years of feeling like he was always the "helper" had left Dennis feeling humiliated and wounded.

Removing some old tile in the kitchen revealed several old layers of tile underneath where whoever had done the work before us had not taken the care to do a thorough job. We also discovered the reason the tile had water damage turned out to be a slow long-term leak coming from the plumbing behind the kitchen sink.

Now that we discovered the real reason for the damage our simple tile job included having to replace rotted sheetrock hidden behind the sink as well as actual cabinetry that had molded and was probably a considerable health hazard.

Like our kitchen renovation it took process to get to the real root of the problem. My father in his later years compared peoples' lives to an onion, which is designed with layer after layer. His life analogy was that each time a new layer was peeled off, yet another new unique layer was revealed. "So it is with us," my father said.

Meanwhile, Dennis was coming face to face with himself. Insecurities that had been conveniently buried began to surface. For the first time in twenty-six years of marriage we were not joined at the hip twenty-four hours a day. Taking summer classes I continued to pay the price for the years I was in college and basically took all the fun classes I wanted. I had lots of units, but not the right ones for a degree, or to transfer, so I continued to take all the required courses I had dodged before.

Occasionally I would try to help Dennis with a project for our home, but the simplest tasks would end with him being frustrated and me in tears. The blinders to much of our own dysfunction that had helped us focus on everything but our own issues for so many years, were being lifted. Dennis clearly resented needing help. Everything made him feel stupid and exposed. I suffered with lots of rejection and was grateful that our daily activities gave us some space.

Signing up for more classes I continued to be amazed at what I was learning and being taught. Dennis and I had a major lack of communication. Many are under the impression that because they speak words, their message is understood.

Here at the local college as I took a class in business communications, I found myself wanting to demand that everyone I knew should have to take this class. The instructor, a fantastic teacher named Lucy, inspired everyone. First, we looked at the different kinds of communication such as verbal and non-verbal. I had to laugh thinking even though what we say and how we say it, is important, what we DO with our lives speaks louder than any words. My mother used to say, "Your actions are speaking so loud, I can't hear what you are saying."

Next the most refreshing news was that the business world in general wanted simplicity, not hype. When I was in high school, teachers taught me that formality and big words were important for business communications and here I was being taught that now clear concise meaningful thought was appreciated. Over the years one of the biggest turn-offs to Dennis and me, when we listened to some teachers, was that they were not themselves.

One day I was watching this grown man, strut all around a stage, using Elizabethan English, and talking at an extra loud volume. I wondered if this were how he talked to his family at home. It seemed so put on and I honestly could not focus on the message he was trying to share due to all the affectations. Why do people think that if they start to talk about spiritual things they need to put on airs? Worse, changing who we are when we talk to someone, we think is important.

Learning about communication, I tried to share with Dennis who was not enthusiastic, about hearing how we could grow. My husband was well on the way down a path of self-discovery that was not a pretty picture. Every devil in hell must have been sent to speak into the ear of this man who had already faced so many challenges. While he was feeling insecure and old, I was starting to be awakened to the fact that we were young and might have half of our lives left. Time after time, I would try to talk about what was going on in my heart and mind and as Dennis was in the process of shutting down, I was awakening and went to the only place I knew to go.

"Honey, I want to go visit Mamma Lori for two weeks."

And in January that's exactly what I did. As a matter of fact, I think it turned out to be closer to three weeks. Dennis was invited but declined and thought maybe a break would be good for us. Arriving in Oklahoma, Lori's son Greg picked me up at the airport. Pouring my heart out about how badly I needed rest, Greg got a funny look and said, "Well Sis, listen to this."

A song Greg had just written played and words about "rest" filled the air and I cried like a baby. It was like these songs had been written for me and enter rest I did.

The next few weeks were spent pretty much in solitude and with Lori. If you have never totally shut out all distractions and just stepped off life's Merry Go Round, you don't know what you're missing. Staying on a fold out sofa in the living room of mammas humble mobile home, I renewed my spirit, soul, and body.

Often waking in the wee hours of the night, I would softly play the special songs that I had first been greeted with on my arrival. Studying for hours and hours, I would get lost in thought and truth. Taking communion and reflecting on all that God had done for our little family, I found myself weeping and saying "If you never did another thing for Dennis or me, what you have done already is enough.

Mamma Lori's nest was so warm and cozy I could have stayed forever. We would awaken when we felt like it, read, study, visit and enjoy the pure presence of the Lord. Peace like a river flowed and time stood still.

Every few days, Mamma Lori would put some amazing homemade stew, and that would be our food for several days. Little did I know the incredible trials that were to come. I genuinely believe now I was granted this wonderful time of preparation for what was to come.

32

Family

Gratitude for family has inspired Dennis and me when life gets hard. The wonderful things that were happening to, and for, our precious children helped us to stay focused on what we felt was most important. Isaac, our first born, had grown closer and closer to a young woman named Heather Dawn.

To our delight, our son's bended knee wedding proposal in the mountains nearby was accepted by sweet Heather. Time was flying and the birth of our first grandson, Evan, was only made sweeter by the realization that there was something incredibly special about his birth date. Isaac and Heather had kept Evan's name a secret until he was born, and it wasn't until a few weeks later we discovered quite a surprise. Evans name is Welsh and Irish for "young warrior."

Before Evan had arrived, I wondered if there might be anything extra special about this first grandchild's birth. Standing in the kitchen several weeks after Evan was born Dennis realized that his first grandson was born on the third month, the sixteenth day and that his name "Evan" is also the Welsh name for "John." There we had it. Evans' special secret. His birth name and date he was born symbolized "John 3:16," the most famous promise in the bible:

> For God so loved the world, that He gave his only begotten son, so that whosoever believes in Him should not perish but have eternal life.

Our precious children Isaac and Heather who had played the song "Show you Love," by Jars of Clay, as the theme song at their wedding during a slide show, had not left a dry eye in the house. Part of the words seemed prophetic, and as anyone who knows Isaac and Heather will attest, they have such an incredible calling to reveal and reflect the beauty of family.

> Speak - and say the words that no one else will ever say
> Love - love like the world we know is over in a day
> I'm gonna show you love in every language
> I'm gonna speak with words that need no form
> I'm gonna give you what you never had before.

In the fall yet another happy memory was made. Although it was unlike his brother Isaac's heartfelt traditional proposal, Isaiah's proposal was unique too, and how should we say... with much dramatic flair! Taking Heather Marie to Disneyland in Anaheim, Isaiah proposed at the top of the "Splash Mountain" ride. Yep! Right before the steepest drop, my awesome son whipped out a ring and asked his future bride if she wanted to "take the plunge." Happy and surprised, Heather and Isaiah became officially engaged.

I had watched through the years as my middle son faced tests and challenges without ever giving up. With spring flying by and the wedding approaching, Isaiah who had been an independent web designer was desperate to have a steady income before he said "I do."

"Mom, I know there is a wedding date set, but I am not getting married if I don't have a steady income."

"Well son, I think you need to shut everything down and spend quiet time. You have done everything you know, so stop and go to the mountains and ask your questions to the one who knows your tomorrows. Sometimes we get so busy handling our own lives we forget we have a loving Father who is just waiting for us to ask for help."

Isaiah headed for the mountains the next day and he truly just stopped to smell the roses. Calling several times, as he wasn't hearing anything specific, I encouraged him to enjoy the scenery and know that whether he felt anything or not, I believed with all my heart things would somehow change.

Late that day when Isaiah returned, he shared he hadn't gotten any great big revelations, but felt at peace. Within a few days he had a thought to check back on a job he had looked at almost a year before that was in our town and was right up his alley.

To Isaiah's amazement, the job was still listed as open on the Internet and he called immediately. First, he was told that the company thought that it had found someone already, but they would send someone to meet with Isaiah anyway. Well, the meeting went so well that the next thing Isaiah knew was that he now had an appointment with the owner. Wouldn't you know it! Isaiah ended up hired locally with a successful web design company who allowed him the time off for a honeymoon even though he was new.

The more we saw Heather the more we knew what a treasure Isaiah had found and couldn't wait for the wedding. Isaiah's Heather Marie now joined Isaac's Heather Dawn making our family more complete. I couldn't have asked for sweeter wives for the boys.

One day, while I was working on schoolwork, Isaiah gave me one of the greatest gifts I have ever received. "Mom, I need you to pick out a special song for the mother and son dance we are having at our wedding." I don't know if my son knows how much his mother likes to dance but the honor of his asking was such an incredible gift.

But how could I possibly share what was in my heart without falling totally apart?

Searching through songs that had been written from sons to mothers, I couldn't find hardly any written from mothers to sons and then of all things, I remembered a song by Rod Stewart, "Forever Young" Listening to the words I couldn't believe what I was hearing.

> May the good Lord be with you down every road you roam,
> And may sunshine and happiness
> Surround you when you're far from home.
> May you grow to be proud, dignified, and true,
> And do unto others as you'd have done to you.
> Be courageous and be brave,
> And in my heart you'll always stay
> Forever young (Forever young)
> Forever young (Forever young)

The words would be literally a blessing, they would speak my hopes for my precious son, and I wept like a baby. I literally had to listen to it for months before I thought I could possibly hear it without falling apart. The wedding had some last-minute challenges and yet sailing through them I found myself dancing with my son in a moment of privilege and great emotion. As the song ended six-foot tall Zay leaned forward and with a chuckle whispered, "Hold tight, Mom!" and making me feel like a schoolgirl again he smoothly whisked me off my feet and twirled me around several times with the biggest grin on his face.

Giving is truly more fun than receiving and the joy Dennis and I had sending the kids on a dream honeymoon, was great. A full week, in Florida, at Disney World. Dennis and I had never had a traditional

Honeymoon, and somehow it seemed so special to be able to give our kids something we hadn't experienced.

The rest of the summer flew by and August seventeenth our precious Sarah who had married Isaacs' best friend Greg gave birth to a beautiful baby girl, Mykayla, who had the biggest eyes I had ever seen. We had an absolute blast picking out some awesome baby girl things. The circle was complete and Sarah who had always wanted to be a mother had her own real-life princess. Now Evan would have a little cousin to play with and the girl count in our family was gaining ground. Hooray. Now with both Heathers and Mykayla, the official family count was boys six and girls five.

The fall flew by and while Dennis continued to work on projects on the house, I took more classes. Since Isaiah and Heather were married our home was quieter and Israel had Mom and Dad all to himself! For years, our home was the hub of activity. Over the years along with Sarah and Trish joining our family we also had shared our home with many others. Each time we opened our hearts and our doors to share what we had; everyone grew.

Now, Israel, AKA "Buck" was enjoying the limelight. Learning to play guitar, he and a few friends formed a band named Farewell Seasons. Dennis and I watched and helped as all the boys grew in life and through the experiences, they were all having. Then as the name implied Farewell Seasons was ready for some changes and the name of the new band was Shelby Snapshot.

Heading for twenty, our youngest son was enjoying life to the fullest and perhaps a little too much. A picture of his dad, this son was going to learn life's lessons by living. Dennis continued projects at home, and yet for some reason, any mention of talking about our relationship as man and wife, what was important and even what the future held caused outbursts and punishing silence. I was starving for true intimacy and it seemed everything I did was wrong. No number of good things happening for our children could erase the pain of feeling so alone even though we lived in the same home.

33

The Gift of Jake

January arrived and I couldn't believe it had been a whole year since I had been at Lori's. The promises I had made with all my heart about slowing down and taking time to make sure my priorities were in order were sincere. But life and challenges had once again started wheels in motion that seemed impossible to change.

Memories of basking in great peace had quickly faded as whatever Dennis was fighting always ended with the same outcome. I was always to blame. We all have issues and my husband truly is a warrior who had overcome so much, and still… this was different. Cutting words would slip out and there seemed to be no restraint when it came to anything in his life.

Israel was still at home and even though we had not had anyone else living with us for over six months, Dennis was verbalizing his need to be alone. For the past year there were some relational things happening that were not making any sense. My husband kept saying he needed to be alone with me, but he never wanted to interact relationally. When we did have time to spend together, he wanted to stare at TV. He didn't want to visit, date, or talk. Forgotten were thoughts about "enjoying" our son Israel's final years at home and concentrating on our marriage.

When Dennis had been delivered of alcohol and cigarettes, he had studied the Word daily. The prayer "Thy will be done on earth as it is in heaven" was what ruled our life choices. We were one hundred percent dedicated to loving and serving others twenty-four seven.

For several years after closing Happy Thoughts my sweetheart kept saying that all we needed was to get away. We got away together, apart, sideways... often he went by himself, three days, sometimes a week. True we had never taken a honeymoon, but if getting away would solve the problem, I knew it should have worked already. Burn out, woundedness, lack of reason, isolation, poor health, and a legion from hell! My knight in shining armor was losing it and there was nothing I could do. Isolating himself he was determined to make it through this battle on his own.

I tried to steer clear and hid by focusing on my precious son Israel who was still at home. I noticed Dennis was not as prone to say mean things when others were around, and I was grateful that my littlest treasure was still in the house. Bringing home lots of his friends I continued to offer our home as a place where Israel's friends were welcome. My son had shared over the years how it meant so much to him, to have a place to bring friends and hang out.

All the boys' friends, homeschoolers and then some could be found eating Mom's tacos and homemade dishes. Neighborhood kids were welcomed, and our home was the center of activity, and I loved it. I was totally convinced that my staying sane was to focus on people who wanted my love and joy and I had decided I could not join Dennis in his depression.

Walking on eggshells, making excuses, and trying to cover for my husband's foul moods, I continued being the consummate enabler, oblivious to what so many were seeing. Over the years I had been trained well and due to major rejection issues thought it was my job to make sure peace reigned in our home. That meant keeping Dennis happy at all costs.

My best friend was in such pain and becoming more convinced that I was the source of all his problems. Blame, anger, and isolation were his friends while exhaustion, confusion, and misery were my mine. I often wondered why I was doing what I was doing, and yet I was sure I was where I was supposed to be and all I knew was I seemed propelled from event to event and there was great comfort in feeling useful.

Dennis and I were invited to Evans first birthday party where Isaac and Heather had the most wonderful surprise. After Evan opened all his gifts, Isaac handed a small little box to Evan and proudly said that this was from Heather and him. As Evan lifted a little t-shirt out of the box, we realized it said something.

"I'm a big brother!"

I remember screaming and laughing and the whole room was filled with people clapping and saying, "Congratulations!" Here in the middle of our trials, was one more reminder of how much Dennis and I both had to battle for as a couple, and as parents.

Ask anyone from split families: holidays, birthdays, and special days, are never the same after a family is split apart with their parents' divorce. Here in our faces was the reality that our children were being blessed and needed us now more than ever.

One day Israel walked into the house and told me about a new friend he had made that he wanted me to meet. Israel made friends easily. Some he told us about and some he didn't, but this was different. "You need to meet him mom. Jake's mother died of cancer and it really messed him up." Israel has always been a great judge of character.

Israel had no idea I had been praying for him to have a best friend. Not a perfect friend, just sincere like Israel. Israel had been venturing out into his own tests and trials. I knew those he chose as friends would have great impact on his life.

While going to school at the local college, Jake had moved into Visalia and the boys were hanging out more and more. One night the boys went to the coast and this new friend poured his heart out to Israel.

My son shared how meaningful it was to him that Jake had trusted him. I was so grateful for this new friend that sensed what a good man Israel is. Despite Dennis and me being such a mess, the answers to prayer in these other areas of life helped my sanity.

One day Israel busted through the door.

"Mom, this is Jake!"

The young man that greeted me had the most contagious genuine smile. Eyes that reflected brokenness and pain could not drown out a childlike exuberance. Tall, over six feet, and obviously of Scandinavian heritage, Jake stuck out his hand with great respect but didn't seem to mind the motherly hug that came quite naturally.

Over the next few weeks, Jake came and went often and even Dennis found himself wanting to support this young man in any way he could. One day Dennis, Israel, Jake, and I were downtown. I believed it was time to share in my heart I felt like a surrogate mother, and to my amazement in response to what I was saying, Jake smiled and said, "I know, God already told me!" What a response! What awesome confirmation! Not in my wildest dreams while praying for a great friend for my son did, I ever imagine he would be another son.

One night during a family dinner I shared with all my children that Jake was basically like an adopted brother and I couldn't have been any prouder than if he had just been physically birthed. I seemed to be the only one totally blind to the age and size of this "new baby." Once again, my other children, including Sarah, gave a hearty welcome to our new "gift."

Jake is talented with lots of construction skills and has a beautiful way of sharing his ideas. When I saw him work with Dennis, I was amazed by how well they worked together. Here I was taking all these communication classes and somehow after years of watching Dennis get so frustrated when working with others, he was spending hours with Jake on projects without any problem.

I realized there was much I could learn from watching the two of them interact. I had picked up habits that were hurting Dennis and it had never occurred to me. For so many years I had been asked to be the "technical" part of the project. Knowing how quickly Dennis would get frustrated when dealing with new things, I had started communicating in a way that was very hurtful. I sincerely did not even think about my delivery and thought I was doing Dennis a favor by being "brief" and not wanting to be questioned!

One day Dennis and Jake were working together when I was in the room and Dennis forcefully was telling Jake how they were going to "do this next step" of the project. My eyes met with Jake's and we both knew that what Dennis was proposing wouldn't work. Had it been me I would have interrupted with "No, you need to do this or that," which would have led to an argument, and further hurt.

The way Jake handled it was, "I had an idea too, but let's try yours first and if it doesn't work, I was thinking maybe we could…" and then Jake explained his idea. Do you know that Dennis got totally quiet and said, "Why don't we try your idea first?"

Standing there flabbergasted all I could think of was all the hurt feelings we both had suffered during projects. Some of this was partially due to the "habit" I had gotten into of mowing over him to get to the bottom line, to save us both time and energy! Wow!

Granted, he also had gotten into a habit of not wanting to "listen or hear" and had his own issues, but I knew now more than ever that our new family addition was being used in some amazing ways.

34

"The Trish"

As all the challenges were happening with Dennis and me, our precious best friend Trish was on her own journey as well. Having been in Texas for several years, Trish found out as we did that life was throwing her some surprises and found herself in a horrible relationship.

Married to a man who had put on quite a front, to her horror she eventually found he had been unfaithful and had been so calloused as to have numerous relationships all at one time. The worst part was that the emotional and mental abuse she had received kept her wondering if she was just imagining things, or truly to be blamed for his unhappiness.

Flying out to Trish's wedding to meet this man we knew something was very wrong. Trish had asked Dennis to give her away and I was maid of honor. My precious friend absolutely glowed and looked stunning. I was to find out a year later that on her wedding night she had been taken home to an apartment that was literally knee high in trash.

Our Trish, trying to look on the bright side, decided this man just needed some help. What do you do when someone you love is set on a course you profoundly disagree with? We decided to support her, trusting that if what we were sensing was real, there must be some bigger life lesson happening here.

The enemy isolated our friend and before long I would get calls where Trish was literally whispering, so her husband would not hear her, or else he would tell her to hang up. He didn't want her talking with others and was very controlling. Heartbroken we watched as our friend who deserved and needed so much tender care had been snared by loneliness and conned.

To keep a charade going for legalistic doctrine and appearances sake can be sick! Our friend spent two years making sure that she was not easily walking away or giving up. On her second wedding anniversary she discovered her husband was being unfaithful again. He was literally online on the computer with another woman while talking to her over the phone about the anniversary card she had given him that morning… that did it!

Answering the phone, I wept with my friend as she shared her discovery of a few minutes before. The pain she was having transcended the distance and moaning I literally had to hand Dennis the phone. Once again, the heart of the man I so admire, came to the forefront while forgetting his own challenges.

"Trish, you hear me. Come home! We love you! Pack your car and let us know when you are on the road. You don't need anything. Don't worry about a thing."

As Trish headed out, we reserved her a room halfway between Texas and California so that she could stop at least once for the night. Trish was emotionally and mentally exhausted and fragile.

Upon arrival at the motel, the desk clerk, who was in on the surprise, acted like we had paid for a regular room and instead Trish found a spa room, flowers and a gift basket. Later Trish shared how words could not ever express what she found. Miraculously sleeping despite all the pain, she found the strength to walk the hard, lonely painful days ahead.

With Trish still on the road we had several days to prepare, so we scrambled to do all that was placed in our hearts. Dennis carefully painted the back bedroom and after that we headed out to a yard sale to find a matching wing chair and reading stand. Moving in a bed, we even bought new sheets and pillowcases to match the comforter and finding the matching mauve wing chair we put lavender highlights throughout the room.

When my mother heard that Trish was coming home, she offered the perfect lamp for reading and a few other odds and ends. Completely decorated down to silk flowers across the top of the curtains, we filled the private bathroom with a giant gift basket filled with bath goodies that had pictures of the ocean. Our friend absolutely loves the ocean so even a special new shower curtain with Tahitian bungalows was hung with great love.

BUT...something was still missing. Going to a local farmers market Dennis and I bought a dainty lavender bird cage complete with a gorgeous sky-blue parakeet.

Complete with candles, two dozen fresh roses, a welcome home card and even a mini fridge stocked with the finest health foods we added the final touches. A special teddy bear waited patiently sitting in the middle of her bed holding the welcome home card in his paws.

Trish arrived at our house and we were so happy to see her home again. Our wonderful friend was close to a complete physical and mental breakdown from the abuse and here in our home her final cares were removed.

"Trish," Dennis excitedly said, "You are here to rest, and you are to rest. Completely! We recently had an increase in cash flow and don't worry, we will cover your bills, and give you spending money for three months."

Seeing the love and care that had been poured out, Trish wept. My prayer was that she would never believe she deserved abusive treatment ever again.

I was thrilled for some long overdue female company and we were able to give Trish the gift of a safe-haven and nest. Not could I ever imagine that I would be needing one of those in the not so far away future. The healing that was accomplished during the summer was unprecedented.

How many times when our own crises threatened to swallow us up, did Dennis and I find common ground helping someone else who was hurting? Now with plenty of diversions, Dennis and I were at least civil and with focusing on everyone but ourselves there was the faint hint of peace in the air.

35

Reroofing and Repairing

With Israel and Trish both in the house it seemed to help Dennis be on his best behavior. Wondering what on earth was happening in the bigger picture, Dennis and I refinanced our home and planned to reroof the house in the summer. Jake, Israel, Trish, and even William from Texas were all part of the plan.

Meanwhile Trish and I were both catching up on some desperately needed girl time. As Trish and I both were awaking up to the fact that it was ok to be individuals, we both realized we had seen enough television and wanted to live life, not watch it.

Jumping at the invitation to play tennis, walk the track and tackle the enemy of laziness and apathy, Trish, and I both couldn't get enough of mothering Jake and getting in shape at the same time. It seemed for Trish and I that when life got rough we never would take care of ourselves using our partners as an excuse for our choices.

Spiritually it felt so good to pour out again to Trish and to Jake. I was realizing I had another good 30 years or so and I didn't want to spend it watching life go by. Trying to be sensitive to what Dennis was going through, Trish and I would invite my husband everywhere but he was not having any of it. One moment he thought things were ok and the next he believed all our problems were simply because his fifty-three-year-old wife didn't want to settle down and she was going through "the change."

Dennis seemed oblivious that during this time, he was bored to tears. The delay of some of our dreams seemed to be catching up with this veteran and even though the world had freed him from a normal job, Dennis wasn't sure what he wanted.

William couldn't arrive until the end of May to re-roof the house and in central California the temperature was heating up and so were the emotions. Isn't it funny how what is inside boils up to the top when great heat is applied? As the heat soared, Dennis and William did not see eye to eye. Meanwhile faithful Jake was helping between working several jobs and even Trish and I were wearing out from trying to be "roofers." Israel helped when he could, but it seemed that Dennis and William were now left with most of the work.

Frustrations aside I now look back and remember some of the events of that time with great humor. Just try to picture Trish and me up on our roof tearing off shingles. The neighbors were now sure our family was nuts. Here were a couple of women both over forty roofing a house,

One day William dropped one of the nail pullers down inside the attic of the roof. Since I was in the house getting water, the guys thought I should go into the attic from the inside to retrieve the tool we needed to help remove the shingles. Jake said,

"Mom, when working construction, we would put baby powder on ourselves before going into an attic to protect us from the insulation."

Sure! Laughing, I now pictured myself looking like "Poppin Fresh," the Pillsbury dough boy or even better, like "Mr. Stay Puft" the marshmallow man from the movie "Ghost Busters." Not quite sure that I wasn't falling for some joke on me, I found some baby powder and covered myself from head to toe. Poking my head out the front door, I announced to everyone on the roof that I was now ready for the great excursion into the attic.

Before I could turn around, I saw the nail puller I was supposed to retrieve thrown down in front of me on the lawn and everyone on the roof had a great laugh as they had figured out a way to retrieve the tool without the need for me to go into the attic. This started a running joke between my new son and I and on more than one occasion when in our home he would be the recipient of a "baby powder" prank when least expecting it.

Our dream to provide extra income for all and save money was turning into a race to finish the roof project before we all died from heat prostration. The electric company decided to double their rates that very month. We literally had the roof off and a one-month electric bill of over seven hundred dollars added to the pressures of the job.

Jake accepted a job running a hay ranch in Nevada for the rest of the summer.

"I'll be back for school. I think this is a good opportunity."

I heard the words, but I was worried as I had seen what a calming affect Jake had on Dennis. He was going to be missed by all and more changes were to come.

Our friend Greg (Mamma Loris' son) arrived in the middle of the reroofing and once again I was hopeful that he would help Dennis somehow. My husband's generosity showed through as he threw Greg the keys to his Harley and told him feel free to use it whenever he wanted while he was in California.

Greg loved to ride, and I was elated that the two were spending time together. Greg was one of the very few that Dennis had ever considered a friend and I knew he might be able to figure out what was going on with Dennis.

The more Dennis sensed that change was in the air he would struggle more and more even though the old ways of doing things were just not working anymore. The freer I became the more Dennis tried to manifest "control." Barking orders and demands, my Honey seemed oblivious that people were noticing.

Years of covering some very dysfunctional areas were now catching up and I was waking up to the fact that I couldn't just ignore what was happening. When others I trusted lovingly confirmed that my best friend was way off base, it helped me to understand that I was indeed seeing and experiencing things that were not okay.

To add to everything else, Trish and I were getting in shape and now that too was a source of anger and jealousy for Dennis. If I could sum up the analogy during the re-roofing time, it would be that like our rotten roof, my husband's mind was worn out too.

Years of life's storms had made their mark and the roof that was supposed to offer protection and safety needed replacing. Isn't it remarkable how often the natural reflects the spiritual in our lives?

While visiting Greg had noticed the verbal abuse and anger that would slip through in the middle of daily activities and asked me how long this had been happening. Sharing that I had been noticing discontent for quite some time I asked our dear friend if there wasn't something he could do. Sadly, he shared that he believed that Dennis was going to have to hit bottom, like he himself had so many years before, and life was going to teach him.

Great! Wonderful! Meanwhile daily I refused to be "bullied" or controlled by the depression and insecurities that were trying to destroy my husband.

"Let your light shine. Stay busy and don't lose your joy!" were my marching orders. All these things aggravated my honey even more. In the middle of this I was given opportunities to stretch and follow my heart, rather than please Dennis at all costs.

Trish and I had both taken summer school classes and when Trish finished, she beamed like a kid getting their first "A." It was so good to see our friend healing and blossoming. She had been so gracious and even though she knew things were really bothering Dennis she continued to support us both.

At times she confessed to wanting to strangle him or me, and yet she believed like I did with all my heart that there was nothing anyone could do but whether the storm. What came next made our friend feel totally betrayed. Dennis had no more to give and honestly believed it was time for her to go. I was so torn and yet remembering years before how he had ended up falling over with a heart attack from the cost his body pays with all the mental garbage, I knew what he was sensing was true.

I was losing my marriage, losing my joy, and my spouse said "I am telling you; Trish has had over three months and a door will open. It is time for her to go."

Dennis was exploding as he was talking, stressed to the max and explaining that he knew he was losing it, and felt like there was no place to be private. The truth was, Trish is very insightful, can read Dennis like a book and the last few weeks had taken to heading straight to her bedroom when at home so she wouldn't come between Dennis and me.

Later she told me that she honestly thought it would cause Dennis to be nicer to me, but I was feeling guilty that the quality of life had changed from wonderful family times to where my friend was feeling as if she had to hide. The truth was, my dear friend had helped us walk through this incredible time of testing, just as much as we were there to help her!

I realized deep in my heart, I had to trust God with my friend, and support my husband. I couldn't believe the timing but knew he didn't know what else to do. He was feeling skinned alive and having an audience watch was just too much.

One morning Dennis shared with Trish in the kitchen that it was time to start looking for another place and it was obvious Trish was incredibly crushed. It was as if, having the total three months, all the tenderness and love put into her little nest, and our wonderful times of friendship, all counted for nothing. It just simply devastated her and there was nothing to do but pray. Within a few days she shared that her old job in Texas had offered her a job back and that with no other doors out here opening, she would take door number one.

Sometimes in life things are just hard and I hoped that someday Trish would know that Dennis was honestly trying to do what he thought was right. Trish was our closest friend. Little did we know that Trish was simply the first in what ended up being a mass exodus from the house so that Dennis could experience being totally alone.

36

Trial by Fire

It was the middle of August and temperatures often over one hundred degrees, which heralded Jake's return to Visalia and the start of school. With Trish's departure, and our twenty-eighth wedding anniversary coming up, I tried to hang on to the non-stop roller coaster that I couldn't stop. Having Israel still at home and lots of company, I was hoping for a miracle. Dennis became more and more verbally abusive and the meaner he got, the more determined I became to "fix" whatever was wrong.

Days before our anniversary, Dennis got mad about something and ended up yelling that he wanted a divorce! Still undaunted, I let things cool for a few days and when it came to a day before our anniversary my husband half-heartedly said something to the effect of, "So, you want to do anything on our anniversary?"

I couldn't comprehend that Dennis really didn't understand how mind bending all of this was, and no matter how I tried to bury the pain, I felt like a kicked dog that would cower whenever its master came around.

Remembering Terra Bella where unconditional love had broken my husband before, I tried to continue to ignore the cutting, heart breaking behavior of a few days earlier and said, "Sure, let's go ahead and celebrate."

Trying to make the best of the horrible year, I decided to totally spoil Dennis for our anniversary. Remembering how Dennis romantically lit a bunch of candles when we first met gave me an idea!

Shopping at a local Marshall's, I found the most wonderful line of candles that individually each had a little leather tie and a little square bronze medallion hanging on each candle. The medallions had the Japanese sign for words like "happiness," "peace," etc. They came in various sizes and I decided that I was going to buy not one, or two… but twenty-eight, one for every year we had been married.

Next, I went to a little store in town called "La Passione" and spent a small fortune on the most beautiful negligee I had ever seen. Inside I honestly didn't even know if Dennis would even be talking to me when the day came but I was choosing to do everything I could to try to let Dennis know I needed him and wanted to work things out.

Reserving a cabin getaway thirty miles away in a little mountain community known as Three Rivers, I also rented a houseboat at the lake close by. As the day arrived, while Dennis and I were enjoying the houseboat at the lake, Israel snuck up to the cabin during the day, and filled the room with the 28 candles, a CD player complete with a custom recorded CD of all of our favorite music, my specially bought negligee, heels, sparkling cider, and a black silk robe I bought for Dennis. A beautiful card completed the surprise.

The weekend getaway was better than I expected, and we talked for the first time in a long time. We talked about our children and life and tried to figure out what on earth had been going on with us. The next morning sitting over-looking the beautiful mountain scenery my husband had Jake on his heart.

At one point Israel had mentioned that he wanted to help his friend out and wished he could live with us! In-spite of the battles within, Dennis asked me if I wanted Jake to live with us! I was honest and said, "Yes!" I had seen the way this young man touched our family and I wanted to honor Israel's place in our home as well, by opening our home up to someone he cared about.

I honestly believed that when Dennis was giving what he could, it helped him stay in touch with the man of Terra Bella who was kind and caring. Arriving home, Dennis took a copy of our book, *Breaking Chains* and told me to call Jake up and invite him over. I did and when Jake read what Dennis had written in the inscription to him, he looked moved! Dennis told Jake, he had seen his character and thought a lot of him and wanted to help him out.

Prophetically, Dennis also wrote that he hoped Jake could handle Dennis's issues. Little did any of us know what was to come. Inviting Jake to officially move in, I felt a breath of fresh air and it seemed maybe Dennis hadn't forgotten everything that we had learned.

After Jake moved in, I was enjoying mothering someone who was so appreciative, and Dennis seemed to be feeling good about himself. Both Israel and Jake were gone a lot with school and work, and I couldn't have been happier with those areas of my life.

Having fun in school and finishing the requirements to transfer to a university made me feel alive and worthwhile. For the first time, I had taken horse-back riding, something I had wanted to do for over thirty years. Asking Dennis to take the class with me, he laughed and let me know, it wasn't even a remote possibility.

Clearly our relationship wasn't about giving, and I started verbalizing a need to go to counseling, a marriage seminar, anything for help. I was starting to realize that it seemed life with Dennis was okay if everything was his way, his timing, and what he wanted! His life seemed to consist of health battles, oldies but goodies, and a desire to watch lots and lots of sports.

I couldn't understand how he could be satisfied with that routine, and yet I still tried to be understanding. Sitting in the parking lot of the local junior college, I listened to Jack Johnson singing about banana pancakes and love. Class was over and I was preparing to go home when I burst into tears and realized my heart was broken. Worse than broken.

I literally had no desire to have any relationship with Dennis whatsoever. As the simple words conveyed the songs message, I wondered what had happened to my girlhood dreams of love and happiness. Literal blinders were lifted and what I saw was horrible. Literally gasping for air, my mind screamed to God questions right and left. What was going on? Why was I so blind? Where had I been?

All I can tell you is that I knew as deeply as I know my own name, this was not just an emotional female moment brought on by the passing of time. I knew I had been given a glimpse of reality and it was devastating. Still questioning, asking what on earth was wrong with me? What is wrong with my heart concerning Dennis and his towards me?"

There were areas in our marriage that were not good or healthy. I guess, neither of us would have dealt with them, without all the pain. Evidently for years, we stumbled along with some incredible dysfunction while focusing on all the wonderful things that were happening with our children, our friends, and our lives. "Change of Life?" Yes! Absolutely!

In the area of respect, ours evidently needed growth and until we saw where we truly were at, we couldn't be helped. If you don't believe there is a problem, you cannot be helped and now, I was forced into facing the fact, both Dennis and I were really messed up relationally and the years of dysfunction had now taken its toll.

Family and friends could clearly see all this dysfunction and now it seemed the time had arrived for home improvements. Crying harder as the words to more songs seemed to point out much that was missing, I just couldn't get past the pain of realizing, I could not fake, cover or fix what was happening in my heart. Slowly driving home, I tried to fight the horrible pain.

Over the next several days I figured out Dennis was wrestling himself and there was nothing I could do to fix this situation! After the initial shock I decided to write a letter, sharing what was going on inside and hoped that he would see this crisis as an opportunity to grow, not fall apart! As I poured out six pages of my deepest thoughts, I could not believe what I was seeing.

I was a first-class enabler and had unknowingly done every classic move to play into horrible dysfunction. No wonder Dennis and I needed to grow, while we were telling the world how free we were, there was this glaring fact, that for people who claimed to have it so together, we still were carrying lots and lots of garbage. We were hurting others as well as ourselves. Dennis and I were about to enter a process that would honestly have us wondering if we would survive. Dennis and I were ready for change!

Writing this incredible love letter to Dennis, I thought there might be an instant change. I thought my heart would be restored and all would be well. Right! No, wrong! I had written down and chronicled what I saw as the true situation, so that Dennis could digest and think before he reacted.

One of the side effects related to being a war veteran was exploding at anything unforeseen and thinking later, so I honestly believed it would be wisdom to write a letter rather than try to communicate verbally when I knew my husband was bound to be defensive.

Rage, anger, and total disbelief might partly paint a picture of the reaction to receiving my letter of love! It didn't matter, that I was so heartbroken, or that I said I was ready to learn how to love and respect each other. All Dennis could see is that he had done something wrong, and that was not ok!

Throwing the offending letter back at me, it was clear, he totally believed I was trying to hurt him. Declaring that nothing was wrong, Dennis yelled that obviously I was crazy, going through the change and I was going to kill him with nonsense. His words? "We are fine!"

Change, communication, and help were all filthy words to Dennis and the fact that his wife was now confronting him added even more fuel to the fire. In my first letter there was not even the suggestion that I wanted anything but restoration and for us to grow as a couple!

My husband's wounded pride responded with denial and disbelief. How could this be? Years before we had been guests on a program named "Back on Course" with world famous Gavin MacLeod, Captain

Stubing of the Love Boat fame... hadn't we ministered worldwide about how to save your marriage? Now, it seemed I didn't even know this angry man who was furious at the truth things were not ok.

As blinders continued to be lifted, I couldn't believe what I was discovering about myself. The hardest part was the realization that I was happier when I was stupid, and blind! Seeing reality was harsh and no amount of wishful thinking could change what I knew in my heart. I didn't know from moment to moment which Dennis I was going to get.

There had been a great cost, being the wife of a "wounded warrior" and I was now honestly suffering literally from secondary post-traumatic stress myself. Years of being kept at arm's length from my closest friend had left neediness, loneliness, and a totally broken heart!

Exhaustion from being the enemy, I had fought, and stood beside, and battled for over twenty eight years with and for Dennis. Now that I needed him, I was accused of wanting to hurt him. It was if all the years of being there for him meant nothing and I thought I would go out of my mind.

One Friday afternoon, shortly after giving Dennis the letter I was told to get out. Packing a suitcase, I grabbed the keys and headed to see a friend in Huntington Beach. Calling once I was on the road, I left a message for Dennis and then called my girlfriend. Thankfully, Joy answered with a warm hello! Asking if she wanted company I laughed and said I was on the way! Simply taking a trip to visit a friend was incredibly liberating. Thinking as I headed south, I sensed the weekend needed to be spent in some girl time and have some fun. A whirlwind weekend included the Long Beach Aquarium, lunch at Bubba Gump's and shopping to boot.

It was so good to spend time with someone who loved to laugh and we both felt like schoolgirls gone crazy! Before leaving town, Joy took me to one of her favorite restaurants and there where you would least expect it, after several days of totally letting our hair down, we ended up having an incredible time together that lasted several hours. We barely could eat, due to the tears and revelation that was shared between the two of us!

Joy who is incredibly sensitive to listening to that small voice inside handed me a page from a workbook she was currently reading. In a nutshell, I was reading an explanation about how wounded people who don't deal with wounds will develop insecurity and allow fear to become a driver in our lives. The fear of being wounded even more, will allow pride and other deceptions to take control of our lives in areas where we should trust. Truthfully, whenever control and manipulation are running anyone, fear, not love, is the driver.

Relating to all the wounds Dennis and I both had been through in life, I remember him angrily exclaiming on more than one occasion, that he would never trust anybody including me! What I was reading seemed to validate what I was walking through with Dennis and the issue of feeling like I was always held at arm's length.

Starting the drive home, I savored the wonderful time with Joy and listening to words of encouragement, I was ready to take on all of hell! That was until a few weeks later. I was now walking a path of loneliness I never would have imagined. I wanted so badly to protect our sons and our daughters, but they honestly were our closest friends.

Isaac, Isaiah, and Israel could only bare to hear so much and tried to distance, stay safe, and not take sides. Dad kept telling the boys, mom was "just going through the change," and yet they really didn't know how dark it had gotten behind closed doors.

The word divorce was now being thrown out on a regular basis and often I was told to get out of "his house." All of this was done when no one was at home, so in the beginning Israel and Jake were spared the worst. I could not bear to hear the word divorce and I continued to give Dennis special cards, write letters, and tried to communicate in every way I knew how.

The more I tried to communicate, the meaner Dennis became. I must have been pushing every button without meaning to, but for the first time, I was speaking up about the horrible things he would say.

Dennis' biggest battle was denial and mine was to stop trying to "help" the situation.

37

Friendly Fire

Do you really think anyone cares
That the fire that burns.... is friendly?

Hearts and body parts
Pieces of promises
Are all being blown away
I need you to see the power you have over me

I know you didn't mean to
But the outcome's just the same
You lean over me, and cry from the truth
You've done it once again

Searing, Burning, Pain I can't control
Someone save me

You didn't mean to do...You didn't mean to say....
The words that shot like fire, through my soul today

Hearts and body parts
Pieces of promises
Are all being blown away

I need you to see
The power you have over me

I know you didn't mean to but the outcomes just the same
You lean over me, and cry from the truth you've done it once again

Kneeling in blood like a child with toys
You cry out to God above
Breathe, Get up, you scream through your pain
I think I've killed my love

The words flowed like a river and I continued to be amazed at how creativity helped keep me sane. "Friendly Fire," the poem I wrote was my daily existence and it was time to admit it… expose it… and deal with it. Writing yet one more letter of encouragement to Dennis I included the words to let him know the condition of our relationship.

Whether writing words to a new song, cooking home-cooked meals for the boys and their friends, or encouraging Israel and Jake to keep playing their guitars, every day was a step into the twilight zone.

One moment my husband would say he wanted to try to change, and the next I was informed everyone was telling him I just had hormone problems, so he felt totally justified in his behavior. I offered repeatedly to go to counseling if he thought I had a problem, but Dennis would not consider it!

There was no way he wanted to talk to any stranger when he was already feeling so betrayed. In his mind, the fact that I was admitting we needed help, meant I was now even more of an enemy than before! Meanwhile, I was getting ready to free me from old rejections while the person I had trusted the most with my heart was going after me with a vengeance.

One afternoon my husband was angry once again and I begged him to calm down. The next thing I knew, he announced he was divorcing me, and would never be back. Coldly packing his special suitcase that fit on his Harley, I continued to follow him around the house trying to talk some sense into him. Frankly, I was so tired from all the fighting and hearing the word "divorce" I hardly protested.

I honestly was surprised that I could even feel pain. I just wanted some peace and knew inside I had no power to fix what was wrong. Following Dennis to his motorcycle I continued to tell him he simply needed a break, and that he could fix this mess. Telling me no matter what else, I had been a great mother to his children, He climbed on his bike and told me I would probably never see him again as the devil would probably kill him if he didn't do it himself!

Walking into the house, again my first thought was gratefulness to God that the boys hadn't seen Dennis saying all these hateful things. My heart still seemed more concerned at how others might be hurt by his behavior. For months I had been covering, making calls, making excuses, and trying not to let anyone know that our home was a war zone. I had quite a well-developed habit of thinking it was my job to apologize for Dennis and explain how he didn't really mean to do the things that he did.

All of that was about to change. That evening, I decided to go visit both sons, who worked at different Starbucks. I knew I could sit home and worry or try to believe that in a few days Dennis would figure out he really didn't want to be away from home or me.

He had already taken off several other times by now, but it had never lasted more than a few hours, and I honestly was ready for a few days rest.

Going upstairs into my bedroom I pulled out a pair of jeans I was particularly proud of. The weight I had lost had allowed me for the first time in years to feel good about the clothes I was wearing. The angrier and more jealous Dennis became, the more I decided to ignore him and continue to try to take good care of myself. Later I discovered this played into insecurities he was already fighting, and it seemed nothing I did was ok.

While everyone else commented on how great I looked, Dennis was critical, accusing me of wanting to have people stare at me for all the wrong reasons. One day as I headed out the door to school I had on a new outfit and was told that I had no business looking nice unless he was there. I could not believe what I was hearing!

Well, I was about to have an epiphany and it was a moment that was incredibly freeing. As I pulled on these pants, I looked longingly at a pair of boots I had only worn one time for Trish's wedding. Along with all the other "restrictions" I had been told not to ever wear shoes that made me as tall, or taller than my husband.

Deciding I needed to feel "special," a "girl thing," I decided to wear these boots. As I sat on the bed to put them on, I pulled one boot on after the other. Just as I was zipping up the second boot, I heard the roar of a Harley motorcycle and without even thinking, immediately started to change my clothes so my husband wouldn't get mad. My first thought was that I would be in trouble if Dennis saw me wearing high heels. I found myself literally shaking so badly, I couldn't get the boots off and then my son Isaiah knocked on the door.

Taking a deep breath, I heard the bike keep going, and headed downstairs to let my son in the door. Asking my son if I looked ok, he answered without having a clue how badly I needed his approval.

"Mom, since you lost weight you have been dressing differently, but I think it's nice."

Assuring me I didn't look "hoochie," my son gave me a great big hug and said goodbye as I ran out the door deciding not to change.

After visiting Israel awhile, I headed out to where Jake worked and happened to arrive just as he got his break!

"Hey mom, I'm walking over to McDonald's for a bite, want to come?"

"Sure," I responded happily.

Walking across the parking lot we laughed and talked about Jake's work, and how his friends were doing. Stepping inside McDonald's suddenly it was like blinders were lifted off my eyes and I literally saw myself falling apart at the thought that my clothing wasn't approved by Dennis.

My God! Here Dennis had just told me for the umpteenth time that he was leaving me, hated me, wanted a divorce and had been horrible emotionally abusive and my reaction? Fear that I might do something that wouldn't please him! Talk about control and manipulation! I saw red and gasping, I couldn't believe what I was seeing.

All I can tell you is I was so angry and for the first time saw how clearly, I had been enabling very unhealthy control and knew that the same demons who had been trying to control Dennis had been doing a pretty fair job of manipulating me as well.

I could not take anymore. Remembering how I used to enjoy a Heineken beer occasionally when I was younger, I stopped off at a Seven Eleven to pick up what my sons refer to as a "forty." That means not small, not twelve ounces. Dennis had left again telling me he was leaving forever, and I knew Jake and Buck were still at work. I think I'll have a pretzel, some beer and sharp cheese! Come to think of it, I was ticked now about everything it seemed. Here I was often not being honest about what I would like, always deferring to what was "good" for Dennis.

Something had always bothered me about the way we would pride ourselves over the fact that we "didn't drink," as if that made us better than someone else. Yes, anything that is done to excess is harmful and you invite addiction, oppression and then possession. There is a path there however and a condition of the heart that is way deeper than those surface actions!

Being sick and tired of feeling responsible for being a guiding light for a man who was now constantly treating me like dung I decided to follow my heart! His choices were his, he was wrestling God, and I was going to enjoy a beer! I did and it was good! I even felt a little less judgmental of many who I had judged.

Two days later when Dennis called to say hello, he made the mistake of starting the conversation by saying, "Oh, I suppose you're having a lot of fun."

No apology. No remorse. No, how are you? The phone call literally started with accusation. The truth was that a bunch of Israel's friends had spent the night to keep me company, and we had all prayed for Dennis and I continued to speak that he was going to be fine, and I was sure he just needed a break.

With the accusation I literally started yelling at the phone and told him in no uncertain terms that I was the angriest I had ever been in my entire life. I told Dennis that if he wanted to depression, anger, and manipulation control his life, that was up to him, but I was not going to entertain any of that!

On top of that I informed him of what I had been shown about his control and manipulation. I screamed into the phone that I would never ever be controlled like that again, and if I was satisfied that what I was wearing was fine, I would wear what I wanted, including high heels! ..."click," Dennis hung up the phone.

The next call two days later was from a humbler man, who said he didn't know why he was riding around in circles and he thought we could work out what ever differences we had at home together! "Come on home," I said without hesitation, "I think we can work this out to too."

38

The Gifts

As the fall progressed, there was a small glimmer of hope in an incredibly dark place! Isaiah had encouraged Dennis and me to go to a "Family Life" weekend marriage conference for quite some time and Dennis committed to going. I was ecstatic and with the hope that admitting we needed help was meaningful, I looked forward to one of my dreams.

I honestly had come to a point that if Dennis hadn't agreed to go, I believed our marriage was over. Up to now, I had a basket filled with wonderful love letters to Dennis, awesome books given to us as gifts, and lots of cards that encouraged we could come through this trial. Well, the basket sat in our living room and most of the gifts in it were never even opened.

Driving towards Monterey, Dennis was acting upset and the knot in my stomach grew as I realized something was very wrong. Confessing that he was honestly furious about missing a big play-off football game, I stared straight ahead in shock.

Pictures of my hopeful, smiling faced boys, waving goodbye as we headed off, ran through my brain and the thought of this weekend being less than a brand-new beginning literally made me sick.

The mother instinct wanted so badly to protect my children from any pain and things kept happening way beyond my control, and they were getting hurt! This counseling was the big effort to save our marriage. I allowed myself some hope that Dennis truly was struggling and not some selfish monster. Now on the road, to the very first effort in over 28 years of marriage to invest in us, he was pissed-off about missing a football game.

Wow! Excuse me. Silly, silly, thoughtless, Diana. I hadn't planned to try to save our marriage around a football game.

My husband went on to share that I should simply be grateful that he was showing up, since he was sure I was the problem! Yep, all I needed were some hormone shots and that would take care of all his abusive treatment.

I was discovering he had come more to appease me than for anything else. So much for the dream getaway. Arriving, we unpacked while Dennis asked what we had to go to that night and what the schedule was. I was starting to feel like the only reason he was here was because it included a "date night" and he was hoping to get lucky. I know that's a horrible thing to say about a married couple, but I finally was learning it was too destructive for me to try to fake wanting to have any physical contact with Dennis.

We were not friends. We were not having any communication, and usually after a particularly abusive emotional episode, Dennis would want to reaffirm his claim on me by getting physical and I just couldn't do it anymore. For the first time in our marriage, I allowed myself the right of not feeling responsible for Dennis's happiness at the expense of my own soul.

I had heard of women who had used emotions and their bodies to manipulate and punish their husbands so for years, I had bent over backwards to make sure that no matter what was happening in my heart, I took care of making my husband happy. I am not kidding…after all… in Terra Bella I had learned that love never fails.

I can honestly say there were times when my heart was so broken from unkind words, I would beg God to get them out of my head, and when they wouldn't leave, I would make love to my husband anyway even though inside it was killing me.

I was now seeing how dishonest I had been, in trying to please Dennis, and he had unknowingly become an idol. For truth to prevail, it was time to get honest and real about every area of our marriage. I guess the question is, what is real love? I was finally realizing true love would be honest, and I needed to let Dennis know how I was doing whether he wanted to hear it or not.

These truths were hitting my hero at the core of his masculinity and yet I was literally sickened at the thought of going from hearing the word divorce one moment, and then being told I should be "in the mood" the next.

So here we were at a weekend devoted to communication and I would have to be honest. Honest with the man whose approval I wanted more than anything in the whole world. And all my disclosures were causing us both, great pain. I never thought of myself as a dishonest person and yet here I was discovering I had been horribly dishonest by constantly ignoring my own feelings.

Ignoring Dennis' grumbling we found ourselves sitting in the Friday evening conference laughing our heads off. The speakers were great and as they handed us the work booklet for the weekend I was thrilled. "Weekend to Remember" was the name of the conference. These people spoke my language and everything in the booklet addressed the issues both Dennis and I were discovering. Opening it I saw the sessions focus.

> **Five Threats to Oneness**
>
> - The first threat is difficulty to adjustments,
> - the second threat is for couples to enter marriage based on performance,
> - the third threat is failing to anticipate selfishness,
> - the fourth threat is our response to trials
> - the fifth threat is affairs whether they be family, or career, or activities, or love.

The results of not knowing how to deal with these. ISOLATION!

Hadn't I been trying to tell Dennis this was happening? He was threatened by my going to school, growing older, and our children leaving home. His reaction to these events was a textbook response of trying to fight change as if change was a dirty word.

This conference was designed so that after the speakers shared, we wrote down our responses to what we had heard separately and then come back together and share what each other had to say. I was so ready to solve our greatest problems and wipe away what was standing in between us.

Saturday was date night and much to my surprise Dennis discovered that the game he had been so concerned about was going to be on. Knowing that it was our date night, he laughed about finding out and then said he was willing to humor me and go on a date instead of watching the game he wanted to see. After getting dressed up in a brand-new outfit, my husband noticed and said how nice I looked. He even complimented the little black high heels I was wearing.

Strolling along Monterey's famous Cannery Row, I had envisioned a dinner at my favorite seafood place, Bubba Gump's, but as we walked along, I noticed across the road, a Pizzeria with a giant big screen with guess what on it? The football game.

Weren't we both struggling with so much and trying to survive this process? Taking Dennis's hand, I steered him over to the restaurant, and seeing the big screen he looked surprised. "What? I thought we were going to get a special dinner at Bubba Gump's," was his reply.

Batting my eyes at him I said, "I'm in the mood for football and a big, long kiss!" Grinning from ear to ear like a little kid, my sweetheart discovered that the game they were showing was the one he wanted to watch, so ordering from the menu, we both curled into the booth to watch the whole game. Slipping my leg over his under the tablecloth in the booth, I continued to surprise my husband with a clear sign of a promising evening, and snuggling closer, the message was clear. The rest of the evening was wonderful and after an intimate evening hope still existed in our hearts.

39

Highway to Hell

Peace lasted two days until Dennis made it abundantly clear he had no intention of applying what we had talked about at the weekend. My husband thought it was miraculous that he had done me the "favor" of even showing up for the seminar. He felt that was worth him being left alone for another six months. After all, we didn't have any problems and I simply needed more hormones. On the other hand, I wanted to be on the same page and was tired of the roller coaster ride! The conference for me was a last-ditch effort to see if he even wanted to address the fact that we needed help.

I didn't like the answer I got when only two short days after coming home I tried to pick up our special books and broached the subject of communicating about our marriage, maybe finish all the parts we hadn't, etc. Screaming divorce from the top of his lungs, I was assured that he had no intention of counseling, working on anything, and I better well like it or get the hell out! I was ruining his life by bringing up these problems and his solution was to ignore them and they all would go away!

With Christmas only a month away, I was told to put on a charade for the "kids' sake." We would talk about how we were going to end this once and for all after the holidays. Because if I didn't hide all this from the kids, I was the worst mom in the world!

Nice. Convinced now that I was living with Dr. Jekyll and Mr. Hyde, I decided to simply do just that. Thumbing my nose in the face of all this strife, I bought all of the married kids presents from the conference aimed at keeping the romance in their marriages and spent my time making the house extra nice for Christmas.

Taking a job at a local Applebee's restaurant, I decided to get out of the house even more and simply stay away from the "friendly fire." The less I was around, the less I could be emotionally bruised. There was always a host of hurting people who really seemed to appreciate the love and joy that I wanted to share with this world. Dennis wasn't wanting anything to do with his wife, so by golly, I continued to look for opportunities to try to bring others some joy.

Spending New Year's Eve away from Dennis I awoke in the mountains to a new day and the smell of fresh fallen snow. I remember it as if it were yesterday and the sunlight was so bright. Ice crystals glistened and a soft wind pushed new snow off the tips of the evergreen branches that had been freshly coated the night before.

Walking towards the lodge where I could get a cup of coffee, I was hit with such sadness that Dennis wasn't there to share such a serene, peaceful, magical moment. As I walked, I realized that taking the job at Applebee's had not helped what Dennis was going through. He was crying out for help with his words and actions and I was adding so much busyness that I was convincing him I didn't need him at all!

That really was not my original intention. I was constantly trying to check my heart and make sure that my choices were not being mean or spiteful. Arriving at the lodge I called Dennis and let him know that I was going to quit Applebee's as I knew it upset him and I knew how much stretching we both were doing. I told him as soon as I was home from the mountains, I was going to tuck in and watch the football games with him. He didn't really react like I thought he would, but I was determined to show support in any way I could without being dishonest.

With January started, I waited to see if Dennis was serious about separating, or if he was just venting yet again. Classes at the local college started up and one day on campus I discovered that there was a part-time job in the counselor's office. Begrudgingly I took the job, as we needed the financial help and working twenty hours a week helped me to try to hang in there for Israel and Jake. At the time I accepted the offer I had no idea what was ahead and had pictured one of my own personal worst nightmares, a boring office job.

All my grown children were struggling through this horrible, horrible time of testing and refining. Israel and Jake knew that things were bad between Dennis and me but thankfully, they were at work and school a lot. Dennis spent a lot of his time at home either parked in front of the TV, or by himself upstairs in the bedroom, where no one would bother him.

Israel was talking about possibly moving out in the fall and Jake was taking about moving away in June, so I was determined to outlast both the boys! I felt so responsible for offering Israel and Jake a warm home, and there was no way I was going to strand them. Running from school to work, and home to cook meals, I simply tried to lay low, leave Dennis alone, and put up with his foul moods.

As my birthday approached, once again my husband exploded over something and informed me that I would be celebrating it "alone." You know, when the going gets tough, the tough get going. Israel just happened to be in a band that was going to be playing up in the mountains at a camp, so I decided to try to make the best of the occasion. Calling a young lady who I had adopted like a daughter, I also made plans to go from the church camp over to the coast for a few days.

I was starting to spread my wings and it was very empowering when it came to where I went and what I did. Everything had always been around Dennis. His syndrome, his health, his moods, his need to be kept busy! I somehow had become probably the biggest stumbling block to the very growth that was needed.

As blinders continued to be lifted, I still had trouble believing how blind I had been. Friends and family were brutally honest and suggested that I had helped make this mess and encouraged me to do what I needed to for peace, yet never was giving up an option from any of them.

Preparing to leave Visalia to drive to the mountains, I decided I wanted to celebrate my birthday with a special drink. After all, here I was celebrating my birthday by myself. Heading into the local Albertsons, I bought some Mikes' Hard Lemonade, or maybe it was Jose Cuervo's pre-bottled margaritas! God knows! As I was checking out, there stood my beautiful daughter in-law followed by my son Isaac! Saying something about how I was headed out of town, I could have sworn, I saw a look of surprise on Heather's face. Mercifully neither one of them said anything, and yet I could hardly help wondering what my children would think about seeing their mother buying alcohol after all the years we had stopped drinking.

Fire was revealing a lot about Dennis and me, and all I knew was that I continued to try to follow what I felt at peace with deep in my heart. After spending an awesome night, where Israel was, I gave my son a new guitar to celebrate my birthday. Son, I really want you to please use this guitar to bring some joy. Then heading to the coast, I spent my birthday day, on a wonderful road trip up Highway One to eat at my fav restaurant and then back to stay with my young friend Amy. We had so much fun, and it was a much-needed breath of fresh air.

Through the spring, the kids and I went to a demolition derby, rode bicycles, walked the track, played tennis, rode horses, and more. Inviting Dennis everywhere I went he would usually say "No" right off the bat. On the few occasions he said "maybe," he always managed to explode before the event came up and then would pout if I went anyway.

I LOVED being around horses and I started playing guitar. Receiving my AA in December, I now was working on transfer units and an AS at the local college. Working at the school turned out to be an absolutely godsend and several precious ladies helped me through some days where it felt like my heart was being pulled apart piece by piece.

One of the most memorable days was when a little lady named Alma, arrived in the counselors' office to see a friend Sylvia who worked there. Sylvia had called me into her office, and she sensed that things were not well on the home front. Arriving Alma handed me a white daisy and mentioned that she wanted to give it to me.

After a wonderful time with the ladies, I hurried home to see what a "white daisy" stood for: innocence and a pure heart. I could not stop crying. If it had not been for many of these little hugs, personal touches to let me know I had not lost my mind, I don't think I would have survived.

Dennis was having an internal battle, and I was catching the fall out. It seemed like whenever there was an exam day at school, that would be a day, that Dennis would end up screaming at me, and it is a wonder, I made it through school.

Sometimes, I would go to the local Save Mart and buy carrots to take with me to feed the horses, at the Ag farm. but carrots was not all that I bought! Sometimes, I would chug a few beers or some other brew and after getting a warm tingling feeling, the pain that was crushing my heart would subside a little! Taking a breath, I would feed the horses, and try to convince myself that everything was really going to be all right.

All I can say for myself is that God is the judge, and my intention was never to harm anyone. I had tried to be perfect and now I saw myself more human, humbler, and incredibly needy.

One time when things had gotten so bad that I had literally slept downstairs in my son Israel's room, my angry husband told us all off, and then went to bed. The next morning, I was awakened softly, by a humbler man with a cup of coffee in his hand, literally in tears. "I have been up all night in pain I cannot even describe. I could feel a small part of what you have been feeling and I am so ashamed," he confessed. He promised to try to get to the bottom of what was going on in his heart.

There was so very much proof that this precious warrior was having a horrific wrestling match, and he was fighting for his life.

I was so grateful for those times of confirmation. On another occasion when I was suffering from extreme torment, I begged Dennis to go for a ride and chill out. Coming home many hours later, Dennis said,

"God told me He has hardened your heart and when it is time, He will melt it like butter." Looking very troubled, my husband also said "I have been warned to stop treating you the way I have been, or I will lose you."

These occasions of communication from Dennis were the beacons of hope that helped me to know that I was not crazy! I was not simply some hormonal woman, needing lots of attention. Repeatedly Dennis would hear in his heart what I was saying in unopened cards, and letters. What a relief... for a few days... and then things would return to the way they were before.

Confused I would ask Dennis, what had happened? When I would try to remind him, that he himself had said he would angrily tell me I was going to make him drop dead from high blood pressure and leave him alone. So, there it was! One moment one thing, and the next, something else!

With the school year wrapping up, Jake was moving up north to spend a season, with his friend Ryan and I had a feeling-things were going to get worse not better. Talking with Israel and his new friend Jaime, I told them I had heard that Yosemite needed stable hands, and trail guides. You received, room, board and pay! With us needing money and Dennis still refusing to get any kind of help, it sounded like a great opportunity for us to get some space. To say the idea wasn't accepted by my spouse is putting it mildly.

On top of everything else, the last year my precious father's health had declined dramatically, and it was heartbreaking. The feeling of abandonment I was dealing with was incredible and I couldn't go to anyone anymore and I needed to get away from the oppression and depression. Three months working in a National Park, sounded like a wonderful break. Against my husband's wishes I determined to get out of the war zone.

Wanting to break the insanity of doing the same thing over and over and expecting a different outcome, I continued to search for answers that would allow growth without giving up all together!

40

Being Broken

It is so easy to talk to someone about their trials, it is another to deal with your own. Not one person on planet Earth has a totally carefree existence, and yet somehow, we all try to escape the inevitable.

Phrases like "liquid gold," "refiners fire," and all the stories of suffering I read as a child were, always portray a loving, benevolent God who says He will never leave us or forsake us, while exhorting us to "endure to the end." These are not words of retirement, and ease!

Surely, Dennis and I were in the process of being broken to be useful for even greater purposes, despite our weakness, and humanity. All I could do was take one step after another in pursuit of peace, joy, and freedom. A wonderful young man named Jason Upton came to our town for a three-day conference and it seemed as if every song, every word, had been handpicked to speak to my heart. Songs that spoke about trusting, and "letting go" ran through the conference songs.

I had a husband not sure of what he believed even though he was hearing I was not crazy and that what I was trying to tell him was the truth. He refused to change anything, and just kept saying, something would change. One day he was saying he would stop the emotional abuse, and the next was back to screaming get out of "His house."

I needed to get out of harms way as physically I was so ill, I had literally dropped over sixty pounds in less than three months. I could not physically stand to eat, as the moment I was upset I would vomit, unable to handle anything on my stomach.

Israel and Jamie thought Yosemite sounded fun and agreed to spend a few months working and living in this beautiful place. Calling ahead, I spoke with a kind man named J.R. who gave us great favor and hired all three of us. Wrapping up my job at the local college and finishing the spring semester of school, I packed my car to head to the new job at Yosemite. Jamie and Israel had headed up a week before I was finished at the college, and I looked forward to some much-needed rest from the warzone at home.

Most of the drive to Yosemite was wonderful. I took some deep breaths and looked forward to having my own space. Dennis was angry that I was going and was fighting losing what he saw as any control over his life or mine. I had purposely turned off my cell phone and played some awesome music enjoying the beauty of the ride to the park. Getting closer to Yosemite, I checked my cell phone and I saw bunches of missed calls from Dennis.

Listening I sat through, the first that said, "Hey, sorry, I was such a creep. Maybe you're right, this break will be good for us, call me!" When I hadn't called back within a few minutes, the next call was accusing, saying I didn't want to hear from him, and by the last call, he was literally screaming, demanding, I call him immediately, or else! Accusations were made that I had not set him up with information to pay the bills while I was gone, etc. and he was going to call our sons to help him since I was so mean!

I had left total instructions, lists, and more, and had constantly reiterated that I could not emotionally take any more stress! So literally the day I was on the road the badgering continued. Convinced more, that for Dennis to start treating me with some respect, I needed to stop the enabling, I waited until I was parked, and called Dennis, assuring him that I was fine, and was not abandoning him. I then told him I would call in a few weeks, have a nice break!

I was going to be sharing a cabin with some nice younger girls and I had hoped selfishly for a cabin to myself! I was told it was impossible and then after totally unpacking into the tiny cabin that held four, I spotted an empty cabin that no one seemed to know about. The office in charge of handing out cabin assignments allowed me to move into it, so after moving all my stuff yet again, finally I had arrived. I wasn't to start work for one more day, as I had to attend a "safety" training class so taking my time I turned my little cabin into a warm nest!

Guitar, harmonica, paints, CD player, you name it, I was ready to call this little cabin home. I couldn't help but notice it seemed like most of the people who worked for the stables had an affinity for lots of beer and late-night bonfires. Israel and Jamie were worried as they had been placed into accommodations into different locations in the park and had heard that "the stables" cabins belonged to the party crowd!

In the few short days they had been there, Israel and Jamie had already gained the approval of the stable bosses and on their day off had managed to go rock climbing with a man who had taught professional rock climbing at another national park! The kids were having fun riding their bicycles all over the Yosemite Valley floor. Even though they were not entirely fond of the hard, hard work, like troopers they were working away and meeting new people.

Less than a week after arriving, my body gave out. A few months before, I had been in an emergency room twice due to severe head aches that caused vomiting that led to dehydration. Here I was in Yosemite with a severe migraine and the nausea was starting. I tried repeatedly to call Israel and Jaime, and since their phones were turned off, I faced the only option, driving home. There is no hospital in Yosemite, and there was no way I was going to be airlifted out the next morning. Praying for strength, I drove all the way back to Visalia, and arriving home, Dennis greeted me with concern saying I never should have gone.

Trying to explain what was happening physically, I headed to the downstairs back bedroom where I had moved and tried to fall asleep. By that evening our home was a warzone once again. By the following day I had an offer to stay with my wonderful sister Chris and her family in Southern California while I went to our wonderful Dr. Moreno and tried to find out what on earth was wrong with my body.

Calls flew back and forth to the kids, and Dennis seemed oblivious to the fact that this was a situation where I needed support. One moment he was yelling, and we both decided, it would be better for me to go through this without him, than to have him constantly losing it. For whatever reason, my husband did not have anything to give in this hour of need.

Hiding out in a bungalow overlooking the Santa Monica basin, I managed to appreciate the surroundings and I walked through the appts with the doctors without fear. One day I took a wonderful drive up the coastal highway from Santa Monica to Malibu! It seemed my life was unwrapping one layer at a time, and the ongoing revelations were sometimes almost more than I could bare.

The day I took the drive to Malibu, I was faced with yet another startling discovery. Stopping at a Starbucks, I noticed a very handsome black man who exuded friendliness. Smiling, he asked for my order, and I realized I was uncomfortable looking into his eyes. Taking a heart check, I questioned God whether I was embarrassed because he was extremely attractive, or was I having a problem, when I realized something even sadder.

The last year had left such wounds, that I was not comfortable looking into anyone's eyes deeply. It had nothing to do with him, or his race, or attractiveness, or my heart! I was simply so wounded that I literally shied away from the contact in fear. My God, this was almost the most shattering of all. I who had carried an absolute gift of joy, was afraid to look another person in the eyes. I noticed the next few days that often when in public I avoided eye contact like the plague! What was happening to me?

While staying with my sister Chris, she kindly confirmed that I was completely responsible for my part of being an enabler and that any time I was ready to stop it… I could! What I love about Chris, is her ability to get straight to the point. With all tests finished, I kissed Chris and her whole family goodbye, assuring them I would take care of myself, and thanked them for the warm hospitality! Preliminary test showed a good possibility of cancer and upon hearing the news precious Israel and Jamie, rushed home to support me.

I can honestly say after all the years of supporting others through physical trials, there is nothing so lonely as facing serious bad news by yourself. There is nothing colder than being alone, in a strange doctor's office where a total stranger tells you it appears you have cancer, a potentially fatal disease. I can honestly tell you that with Jesus, I was not afraid.

Arriving home, I remember finding a card, welcoming me home, and in it my husband swore to try to be calm, and not verbally attack me, and yet in less than one day, he found himself standing in our hallway screaming at me and losing it.

Finally, the news came. NO CANCER! Thank God! If stress affects cells, it is truly God's grace that we received such a report. Dennis was relieved while also saying he would have been furious if the result had been any other, and all I knew was that I was so grateful. Continuing to live in my own room downstairs, I had finally set some parameters for my own sanity.

Israel was getting ready to move to the coast with his friend Jamie, and I decided that I would just live downstairs while Dennis came to the end of himself. I honestly didn't think he could keep up this struggle much longer.

Visiting yet another woman friend, I heard things I was not prepared to hear.

"Let go."

Handing me a printout about letting go, Debbie gently said what needed to be said! I had to confront Dennis, and I had to get on with my life! True trust! It seemed for the next three months everywhere I went I would hear the same message.

Let Go? Let go of what? Myself? Dennis? Marriage? Control? What? How? When?

It was inconceivable to me that after a cancer scare, Dennis still was refusing to talk, communicate or deal with all this mess.

After talking with Debbie, I went and bought a giant bottle of tequila and headed to my dad's empty house, which was for sale, to lay by the pool and think about all that was said. I know now why alcohol used to be called liquid courage.

After doing yard work all day and totally downing the entire bottle over about six hours, I headed home to let my husband have it with both barrels! To say he was in shock was putting it mildly.

"You don't love me! I shrieked! You don't even know me! You are not my friend! You keep saying you want me here and then do everything you can to drive me away!" I screamed at him the way he had at me for years when he was upset, and he genuinely seemed shocked."

You've been living in a television for years and want to die! What are you still doing here? You think God is done using us?" I declared how sick and tired I was of all the lies, false accusation, and how dare he think that he had any right ever to treat me in any way that was less than respectful.

"You need to find out what you believe!" I bellowed louder. I honestly cannot believe someone didn't call the police, as I was hollering at the top of my lungs. Dennis was speechless and he apologized and was nice for a couple of days.

One Sunday, I went to a church with Isaiah and Heather, and I heard the same words again! "Let go." At the front of this church stands a big wooden cross. By the cross, is a basket holding a hammer, nails, paper, and pencils. After the service I fell literally on my face, at the foot of the cross.

Sobbing so hard, I could barely write...there at the cross, I wrote my husband's name, the words covenant, marriage, and literally nailed the tear stained, folded up, piece of paper to the cross. I let go.

41

Letting Go

Trying one last time to find a temporary solution to our need to find some space, I looked for jobs at resorts. Hearing from a hunter's retreat in Colorado, I was promised room, board, and at least two hundred dollars a day in tips from waiting tables.

I had repeatedly begged Dennis to go visit Mamma Lori, or her son Greg, find a campground to camp in for a week, anything, but since this awful time had begun, even though I had heard he was wrestling God, I kept hoping that we wouldn't have to formally separate, or move away from each other.

The home front was just too volatile and no matter what I did to avoid warfare it was coming down the hallway and seeking me out. How I ever finished one class let alone passed with a high GPA can only be credited to my learning to focus no matter how bad the warfare was at home. Packing the truck yet one more time, I noticed Dennis kept accusing me of leaving him. One moment he was yelling at me to get out of his house, and yet when I made plans to take a break, he was angrier yet. By now I realized that I honestly believed I was dealing with more than Dennis.

Driving to Colorado, I spent the night in the truck in Primm, Nevada. There is an oasis of sorts, where you can buy a prime rib dinner for $6.95 and the rooms are only $19.95. The owners are so sure you will drop lots of money gambling, so everything is ridiculously cheap!

Spending a day in Primm, I rested and sadly listened to a group in one of the casinos sing all the best Motown love songs that Dennis and I used to enjoy together. It was getting harder and harder to picture restoration as by now all I could see was accusation, anger, and jealousy from the man who I had once shared so much with.

Continuing to the Colorado Hunting Lodge Resort, I pulled into the front office. I was given a tour by the woman who had hired me, and anxious to get unpacked, I was escorted from the million-dollar lodge to a broken-down laundry room, hidden by some pine trees.

Here someone had placed an old mobile and had covered the sides with fake logs hidden by some trees. There was a door on each end of this little building, and I could see there was no lock on the door I was walking into. In the middle of this "building" was a commercial washer, a few dryers, junk, old food, and a poorly built table that was supposed to hold towels and wash cloths that the "maids" were supposed to wash. To the right was a room, with a twin bed sized stained mattress, no dresser, and carpet with holes in it.

Completing my new "apartment" were the three windows that had glass broken out of with old torn sheets hung across to help keep out the soon-to-come fall rains. It was mid-August, and the temporary job was supposed to last until November. To get to the only bathroom, one had to go to the other end of this mobile and knock on a door to another bedroom, asking its occupants if you could please use the toilet. There was no shower and the young couple shacking up in the other end were so stoned that my first night there, they forgot to unlock the door so I literally had to pee in a plastic trash can! Staring at all of this, once again my attempts at finding peace blew up in my face. Exhausted I called Dennis and told him what I had been greeted with! The words "I knew you weren't supposed to go" stung.

"Come home where you are loved." Right, loved one moment until the other Dennis showed up! Be that as it may, my insides were absolutely churning and packing in the wee hours of the morning, I drove away without so much as a goodbye! That woman knew what she did!

She thought I would be unable to afford the gas home! God forgive her, I have.

Heading home on the freeway I had another meltdown, and finally could take no more. Dennis had called and screaming at him, at God, and continuing to cry out "Why?" I fought off strong suicidal thoughts! What did God want from me?

Wasn't I trying to give Dennis the space he needed? I physically and mentally could not take the roller coaster anymore. My sons didn't want to be in the middle and my mother and sisters were not exactly objective with the pain they had seen me in. Worst of all, my eighty-two-year-old father, my hero was dying. Suffering from one ailment after another, he was on the journey of his body and mind shutting down and not once through this horrible ordeal had I ever mentioned to Him that Dennis and I were having any problems.

For the last three years of his life, my precious father would watch Monday night football with Dennis, and they had made quite the friendship. Dennis enjoyed the father he had not had for many years, and Dad enjoyed a son, after having three daughters. There was no way in his failing state I would have worried him with something he could do nothing about.

So here I was up against a wall, and absolutely shattered. Dennis tried to say a few words of encouragement, but talk had become cheap. Promising to go to a counselor, and swearing we would do whatever it took, Dennis shared that he couldn't believe how heart broken he was after I drove away, and he realized I wasn't kidding. He thought I would be gone for three to four months and he had hit his knees yet again, calling out to God. Hanging up from Dennis I called Trish, and asked her to pray, and cried, and cried, and cried! Driving for hours on end, I made it back to Prim, an deciding that I might as well take a breath, I stopped by for another prime rib dinner, and a room for the night to get some good sleep after the long drive there and back!

I arrived home the next day and Dennis kindly helped unpack the truck and made an appointment to request a counselor from the VA.

I called my poor children who had tried to be supportive through this whole crazy summer. They chose only to welcome me back with open arms. I could not explain why all the tests, why all the doors would seem to close when Dennis would call out to God. I know it seems hard to understand but my only hope and faith, that I was not totally insane, was the truth. From the beginning, I know, that I know, that I know, what God said to me, and I did not want to give up hope that there actually was a triumphant end to this nightmare.

Hadn't I repeatedly let go? What was I missing? With school starting yet again, I signed up for classes and found that if I worked hard by the end of Spring, I could have yet another degree. The VA counselor finally called, and Dennis headed out the door to face one of his worst fears. Why on earth would someone so wounded willingly expose himself to someone else who couldn't possibly understand what he has walked through? We were both desperate for help and I frankly didn't care how the help came. After a few visits to the counselor, Dennis quit, and he still was not honestly ready to change anything. Lashing out yet again, I could barely believe what the last year had held. Neither of us was willing to give up, and yet deep down I knew this trial was still not done!

My husband had realized this past year how little he truly knew about his wife's heart and at one point was willing to even take a horse back riding class with me. When he went, he really did enjoy himself, but the struggle inside surfaced and he would punish me by quitting the things he had committed to. Our lives had been so wrapped up in him that when people would ask me how I was, I immediately went to talk about Dennis. I had become a non-entity.

Surprises of all surprises during the storm, yet another gift from on high! Micah's first birthday was approaching, and few had forgotten how cleverly Isaac and Heather had announced her pregnancy at Evans birthday party. Now a year had passed, and the family was gathered at Isaac and Heather's. After opening presents, Isaac smiling announced, and this is Micah's gift from Heather, and me. As Micah tore the paper off the last package, a magnetic toy for the refrigerator was revealed, and at the same time, a book fell onto the floor that had been tucked in with the toy. Smiling extra big, Isaac held up the book which was a Bernstein's Bear book entitled? AND BABY MAKES FIVE! Here during our worst trials Isaac and Heather were pregnant with their third child. Deciding not to find out whether the new baby was a boy or a girl, we all were in for an exciting Spring!

Looking at Dennis I wondered if this would be a wake-up call of some kind. Perhaps these were little rays of light and hope amid a very dark time for us as parents. Overjoyed I just could not picture our family separated and was sure that perhaps this good news would change my husband's heart. Thanksgiving had come and gone, and Dennis had stayed home and gotten drunk instead of going to the family dinner! By this time, I was honestly not surprised at much of anything. I felt numb most of the time. This was not just any holiday; it was my fathers last outing from the convalescent home, and I was disgusted Dennis chose to miss the time with him and the kids.

Getting up the next morning, I was walking down the hallway to the kitchen when Dennis came from the other direction. The presence on my husband was a ticking time bomb and standing my ground I braced myself for what I sensed was coming.

"You ruined Thanksgiving, now you've ruined Christmas, and we are not going to have any lights this year"!

There was no apology, and I was repeatedly told that there would be no Christmas this year! I remember thinking,

"Is that right"? and in no uncertain terms, I stated this was the last time I would be talked to with such disrespect.

Three days later Isaac and Isaiah moved all my belongings over to my dad's empty house that had been up for sale since he was no longer able to keep it up. I had driven around in circles for three days, depressed at the thought of leaving everything that held any comfort, and finally realized I was being stupid not to simply ask Mom if she minded if I use the house until it sold.

On one hand I was so exhausted from all the moves, and yet on the other, it made sense. "Trust Me" was what I heard, and assuring my sons, that I would not be making any quick moves this time, they walked me through this like the troopers they have always been.

"Sons, your dad has to be left totally alone, and I need to get out of the way. I believe this is going to be worked out, but you are all getting hurt even if I am in the house, so I might as well, go make a nest and let him have what he keeps screaming for!"

42

The Nest

I may have gone kicking and screaming, but I was never surer of anything in my life! It had taken over a year to walk out letting go. Valiantly I had fought what I was hearing, to make sure, very sure, that every other alternative had been exhausted.

My giant gift basket sat in the corner of the living room, like an altar of sorts, full of attempts at communication. Filled with unopened letters, cards, books, and gifts it was a horrific mirror of physical evidence. A picture of my response to Dennis yelling "divorce." Dennis often wouldn't even open the cards or gifts that I would give him, so off they went into "the basket."

Before the actual moving day, I thought about twice before when I almost "let go." I had moved out once to my father's empty house for about two weeks, and when Dennis came calling, I instantly moved home. There even had been a time that I had miraculously found a little nest of a studio, literally by a river, that had horses. My husband had no idea I was even looking and calling our friend Greg, we agreed that if the door was opened, it was time.

The door mysteriously shut and the next day, Dennis had once again said he wanted to "try to get help." All I knew is that truly Dennis and I were being ground to dust and it wasn't very pretty. The hardest most painful part of all was the cost to those we loved!

My children, who had known so much love could not understand why we couldn't just get along! They really couldn't conceive that we were right where we were supposed to be! There was so much pain at the holidays, birthdays, any special event where they needed their parents to be supportive and "together."

Anguish in my heart that Dennis was missing moments with my father that could never be regained! I went through a total spiritual, mental, and emotional divorce. All my life I had preached Jesus was enough and now He had to be! Dennis would be civil for a few days when he wanted something and then the moment he did or didn't get what he wanted; he was back to the same behavior. It really didn't matter whether he got what he wanted or not! The moment the conquest was over, the other guy surfaced!

My mind was so bent, so bruised, and so weary, I welcomed the peacefulness of solitude. Here of all places my nest was in the very home I grew up in! Mom was wonderful and offered to pay me on top of staying there for free, to do the yard work! The place needed kept up while realtors showed it!

My first night all alone, I looked around the room that I had worked so hard to set up. The overhead pastel gold colored glass shade emitted a warm glow that softly lit my new bedroom. Placing the bed in the corner of the room allowed me to stack up pillows along two sides making the bed look absolutely inviting.

Covering the soft king-sized bed was a comforter that had been given to me by Dennis' sister Sheri. A fuzzy, brown, stuffed bear that Trish had given me sat proudly in a corner just begging for a hug. A crocheted ivory covered doily sat on the nightstand under a reading lamp and sitting next to the baby blue lamp was an adorable figurine of a sitting bear dressed in a robe, holding a teacup. Next to that I had placed a hand-tied bunch of lavender to remind myself of a day that Dennis and I had been to the coast.

Walking down the beach a little child was selling beautiful little bunches of fresh lavender and approaching timidly asked if we would like one? To my surprise, my husband barked out harshly that we couldn't afford that, before even knowing the price. The look on the child's face was heart breaking and quickly, I enquired how much? Two dollars was the reply, and buying one, I couldn't help but think what on earth had happened to the man I used to love. He was smashing everything in sight, blind and numb to the results of his actions. Oh, he had money to buy a beer, or a bottle of vodka if he wanted, but there was no money for flowers!

The final item on the nightstand was my Bible. Ironically, there was an inscription from Dennis, encouraging me to grow as God had greater things for me to learn! Well true, there was nothing said about "sharing" what I was learning. Sinking into the bed, such a peace permeated the room, and I pictured our friend Trish wondering if this is how nurtured she had felt at being in her little nest?

Peace, peace, wonderful peace. I knew that I was in the right place and I slept like a baby for the very first night in my new home!

By the second night, Dennis who was losing all control was banging down the door late at night. Dropping off our little dog Frito Boat he shoved his way into the house, and declared I was going to keep the dog for my own safety. Right! A three-pound tiny old terrier mix who had a cataract and was toothless! It would have been funny if it weren't so sick. Ushering him out of the house, I locked the door, and returned the dog in the morning.

Writing yet one more letter I asked Dennis to leave me alone. I will not answer calls! I will not pay your bills! Whether we lost the house or whatever, Dennis was not my problem anymore! The crazy thing, was that he honestly acted like after literally telling me he hated me, get out, and didn't need me, he told me I should continue to pay the bills, and do everything to make his life wonderful! On top of that he was angrily telling his family I had "left him," Yikes!

I refused to be part of all of this and told Dennis any further communication would need to be in writing. I tried to explain literally for our health's sake, all the harassment was not okay, but my husband was out of control. I then added my own demand.

"Until you have talked with Mama Lori, or Greg, I am not going to even consider coming home." Dennis simply could not believe I was following through with what I said!

School was going along, the horseback riding classes for the third semester were wonderful and being in the home I was raised in was such a gift of comfort. Continuing to walk through the process of seeing my dad's failing health, I fought and wrestled trying to somehow make the process better. Taking Dad for wheelchair rides outside of the convalescent home was emotionally hard, and yet somehow strength came. I never will forget a day when I felt led to take dad outside to where the roses were and then I sang for him

My Dad was a shadow of his former self, and yet his eyes still twinkled with light and recognition. When he could still communicate, he had told me that his favorite song was "Oh how I love Jesus" so that was one of the songs that I sang that day for him. God promises to be a father to the fatherless, and truly my Dad, an orphan who had grown up in an orphanage, was greatly loved during his sojourn on this earth. In my adult years, I grew to respect his strength and joy in new ways, and truly it was a privilege to sing to him.

Singing "In the Garden" and several other songs, I was amazed at the strength that I was given to "see" Dad's spirit and not his physical body. Watery eyes and a smile were my reward for the mini concert, and it was wonderful, that knowing here in the stench and indignity of failing bodies, there were moments of love, peace, and joy!

Christmas was fast approaching, and the dumb devil hated lights huh? When I had the boys move me, I had taken all the Christmas decorations, and decided that since Christmas was not about Dennis, I was going to celebrate, and so was our family! Getting out the tallest extended ladder from my dad's shed, I prepared well. Since I was going to the roof top, I carefully put all the lights I wanted to use on the roof into a trash bag along with extension cords, a hammer, and some tape.

Since my father's house is two story, it didn't hit me until I was on the roof, looking down that I must be crazy. A few days before, I had battled through another bout of headaches and nausea, and even had to take medication to be able to keep anything on my stomach. The doctor. simply stated my body was shutting down from all the stress, and even wanted to give me an anti-depressant!

Thanking him, I refused that part of the therapy as I honestly believed having a broken heart during this was healthy. After all, Dennis and I were in the middle of having our hearts torn out after twenty-eight years of marriage and some depression and grieving was appropriate. I was sure that now I was not going to be under attack daily, I would be ok, and I simply needed something for the nausea.

Here I was on the roof that had a very steep pitch to it, with a bag full of lights and suddenly, "super woman" had a fear attack! Laughing, I laid on my back on the roof, and one by one tried to call my children to see if any of my sons might be available. No such luck! No answers anywhere, even from Jake, who had moved back to Visalia, after living up north for seven months! Connecting with Heather Dawn I explained that I was losing my mind but if no one was available I was just going to have to finish the job! Three hours later I had decorated the house with every light that we had ever owned. No lights? HA!

All my children had been invited over for a holiday evening, and we all managed to make the best of the situation! Christmas music filled the house and a beautiful tree with lights glowing like a scene from a Charles Dickens book, greeted the children. My heroes! Asking the kids if they wanted me to invite their father over for Christmas morning, they agreed, and I honestly wanted to make an opportunity for everyone to enjoy the day as best we could!

Calling, I invited Dennis over for Christmas, and shared that we honestly would miss him, and if he could come, and celebrate family, without turning the whole thing into him being the focus, he was welcome! Christmas morning came and went, and the greatest joy that made the day monumental was the good news that our son Isaiah, and Heather were expecting their first baby! Our Isaiah pulled out the bubble gum cigars and passed them out with great fervor. Talk about reminders of promise and hope. How on earth could any of us have any peace until our family was restored? Anyone who has lost a loved one, will tell you, there is a gaping hole that cannot be filled until restoration happens! It is just so! God can fill it, and make the pain go away, but something is still missing!

Ever wonder how God must feel when someone he loves is missing?

43

Standing

As the holidays progressed, the truth was that Dennis was discovering that no bottle of vodka, no amount of Elvis videos, or isolation, not even sitting in the spa for hours could make up for being alone. Months before he had admitted, he did not know what he wanted. He didn't like himself and he sure didn't like this new Diana.

Being alone allows someone to have everything their own way and can be quite a comfy place. Both of us were searching and asking questions, and all I knew was that the same God who had delivered my husband in the beginning had promised to see me through one day at a time, one step at a time.

Since my husband had continually blamed everyone and everything for his life, it was quite a mirror to have everyone removed! No one to blame! No one else's fault. Dennis was given the gift of seeing what his life would be like without me, and that didn't seem to be the answer! Here I had watched as one by one everyone was removed and he was given the ultimate opportunity for selfishness! To say he was not in heaven is an understatement.

After all, he had a pension. I had not taken a dime when I left. But Dennis experienced what life would have been like without me. I specifically chose not to give him any extra excuses to have to blame me for his unhappiness. Wow! Over the years, our favorite movie was, "It's a Wonderful Life," where a kind man named George Bailey gets to see what the world would have been like if he never had been born!

It seemed that once and for all, God had allowed my precious husband to have what he wanted in his heart and it turned out not quite like he had pictured it! So many movies have been made about men who came to the defining moment of giving up pure selfishness. Jim Carey, in the movie 'Bruce Almighty' discovers at the end of the day that true love is when you honestly want what is best for the other person whether it benefits you or not! Dennis was coming to the end of himself and like God had promised him at the river, my heart was starting to be softened.

Broken was the angry raving man pounding down the door and demanding his own way! Gone was the dishonest enabling wife who now had learned the importance of being honest. Never again, hopefully, would I say what was expected just to keep peace. All I knew was I was not released from my best friend; I simply was needing to get "out of the way."

The next two months were an ongoing breaking and finally Mamma Lori wrote Dennis a letter! Sharing that the legions of hell had returned; Mamma wrote a letter sharing her love for Dennis! She told him to be free and enough was enough!

Several weeks after getting Mamma's letter, Dennis called and spoke with his spiritual mamma for the first time in years. After that he called his best friend Greg. Dennis actions were finally lining up with his words, and he shared that he was sorry for all the choices that had hurt so many.

In February, of 2008, four months after I had moved out a humble repentant man stood at the door. Sharing he was so ashamed, and would wait forever if it took, it, he apologized, and asked me to think about coming home.

This was not the manipulative, demanding angry person who had been in the middle of a wrestling match. Thanking him for the invitation, I waited a few more weeks. My heart had been melting, and I saw my husband through the eyes of the one who made him and I knew he was sincerely changed. Dennis personally packed and moved every piece of furniture, everything with tender loving care and together we started the long hard work of healing, restoration, and simply trying to understand what we were supposed to do next.

Telling me that he wanted to write from his heart, about our separation, my wonderful husband shared below his thoughts and memories of such a hard time.

Dennis:

"Dennis you will not abuse me anymore!"

"What are you talking about?" I asked. This was a total shock to me. I knew I've always been kind of controlling, but I always looked at it as being humorous or funny. I found out that it was not all that funny to my wife and kids. My wife shared this was extremely mentally abusive. In my mind I diagnosed the problem as Diana going through the change of life and that I have always loved her and my boys more than life itself. With all the years of care providing, which is totally giving of yourself mentally and physically, plus raising our sons at the same time, there wasn't a whole lot of time for Diana and me. Deep down jealousy for more of her attention was part of what drove me to treat her less than kind, also my issues from Vietnam and being an ex-drug addict and alcoholic.

All we both knew was we had to be apart before we damaged each other beyond repair. So, Diana left and went to live at my father in-laws, empty house. Oh my God! Reality hit. It was probably the most painful time we have both experienced in our lives. But at the same time this is something that had to happen. God knew what He was doing. We gave our whole lives to Him in 1978. We did whatever we thought we heard Him say to do and went where we believed He said to go. I personally believe I was so exhausted spiritually and physically that I just said screw all this religion. I am going to drink again, the kids are moved out, my wife has left me, I'm going to do something for me! The door was wide open for a big pity party all right! Well the devil had me right where he wanted me. I always try my best to be honest. It was fun for a season, and then I found out life is not the same when you have beautiful children, a beautiful wife, and you owe Jesus everything for all He has done for you and your family.

For all of you men out there going through the change or for whatever reason feel the need to act out your youth again, I'd just like to say, be patient with yourself, and your wife and kids and the Lord will help you work things out. He promises to do that.

I'm seventy years old. I was sober 25 years and then the pressures of life led me to break.

The joy in my life still and always will come from the understanding and unconditional love of Jesus Christ, my wife, and my sons, and daughters. I am very blessed to have my family stand by me in my time of darkness. But my darkness didn't have to be if I hadn't been blinded at what was standing right in front of me. I hope you do not choose the path of giving up on your marriage and that you would stand up and fight and keep what belongs to you, your family! I'm so grateful my family forgave me and I have a second chance.

The Nickell family

...and Isla Harmony, makes nine!

44

Thirtieth Anniversary

Diana:
Israel and Jaime had moved home in early February, and once again, I could not help but be in awe at how giving Dennis could be. In late January, Dennis and I had visited the kids at the beach and discovered that they were coming to a turning point in their lives. While going to school on the coast our son had left school to work for a man who owned a coffee company. Offering Israel, a partnership, it seemed like our son's dreams were coming true. His years of experience were paying off and he was offered a real co-ownership if he would help to open a second coffee shop.

Often working seven days a week, he was so excited to have a real shot at success, until he figured out, he wasn't being paid for his work. Meanwhile Jaime had finished another semester of school and both had discovered that when you work at the beach it seemed like you rarely had time to enjoy it!

Hearing the kids' thoughts Dennis immediately offered for them to come home and have a place to be while they resettled in Visalia. Things had not worked out quite as they thought, and since my husband had figured out that other people were not really the root of his problems, he thought it would be nice to have the kids back.

As anyone who knows me will attest to, I am normally in my element entertaining others, and whether it is making nachos for the masses at 2:00 a.m., or visiting with our kid's friends, I always looked forward to good company. I really looked forward to getting to know the young lady who we all thought was destined to be our daughter in-law. Jamie had been through some battles in life and thankfully had a "feisty" attribute that would equip her well for dealing with my son's tenacity!

Around the same time, our newest son Jake had confirmed that he had met someone extra special that he knew was "the one." He and his Esther just could not stand to be apart, and when Jake told us he was thinking of inviting her to come to our city to live, once again he asked Dennis and me to meet her.

Dennis and Diana

Esther! This young lady turned out to be everything Jake had said she was! Meeting in Fresno, Dennis and I shared what was on our hearts for them and invited Esther to move in with us to be in the area until she and Jake got married.

Meanwhile our wonderful pregnant "Heathers" were both due soon, one in June, and one in August.

As our thirtieth wedding anniversary approached, we knew It had been an incredibly hard two years filled with life, passion, and growth for all our family. While Israel proposed to Jamie one way, Jake proposed to Esther another. Somehow our family had survived the worst of an unbelievable process that reminded everyone of us what on earth is important. As our wedding anniversary approached, Dennis and I had no idea the final surprise in store for such an incredible summer.

When Isaiah and Heather found out she was pregnant, they were able to buy my fathers home, the house I grew up in. With help from my mom, they were able to jump through all the hoops, get a great deal, and keep this wonderful home in the family. Heather, now a licensed RN wanted to have a home birth, and to our great joy, On August 22nd, 2008 just a few moments before midnight, Brock Thompson Nickell entered the world literally born in his great grandfather's house on our thirtieth wedding anniversary.

New life....and the story goes on........

EPILOGUE: IF YOU ONLY KNEW

by Diana Nickell

If you only knew!
Fast forward time
To the days that are fine
Where laughter replaces the screams.

Fiery trials
Challenges and pain
Diminish with the passing of time
You laid the gun down
With no hope in sight
Thinking of others not your own plight

This one small act
The gift of time
Not giving up or committing that crime
To swallow the lie that there is no hope
Just a victim that cannot cope
Would rob us all of your treasure

You decided to stay
Just in case there might be,
a different ending that hasn't been seen
YOU'RE RIGHT!

EPILOGUE: IF YOU ONLY KNEW

The second you looked
For the next open door
Circumstances start changing
No one can explain
Moment by moment

As time passes on
Perspective and wisdom arrive
This man with no hope
Full of demons and rage
Never knew what his future would hold

Yet step by step
he refused to give up
Help came in miraculous ways
By the time the picture was taken
Of the old wise veteran above

He had 37 years of his best friends love
Sons that he admired
And learned how to father
Their wives were the daughters he loved

EIGHT GRANDCHILDREN STRONG
With one more on the way
She arrived six months before the day
The day that Dennis
Left this earth and entered eternity
He left a trail of love and friends
Changed lives and so very much more

So next time your reaching

EPILOGUE: IF YOU ONLY KNEW

For a pill or a gun pondering taking your life
Wait... take a breath time doesn't stand still
Each morning wipes the slate clean

If you only knew
What could be your future
The joys that wait for you
You would reconsider it's true

Dennis and Diana